A WOMAN fulfilled

A WOMAN Fulfilled

MARILYNNE TODD LINFORD

BOOKCRAFT
Salt Lake City, Utah

Library of Congress Catalog Card Number: 92-70189

ISBN 0-88494-823-4

First Printing, 1992

Printed in the United States of America

Contents

Preface

On one occasion I talked to a friend who has a loving husband, cute and wonderful children, an expensive home, more than enough money, and a beautiful face and figure. Despite all these advantages, she had a laundry list of worries, complaints, rejections, fears, and trials. I thought I could joke with her. I said, "You sound like a latter-day book of Lamentations." As though I had said nothing, she continued: "I feel so empty; I don't even know how to begin to fill up."

I asked her what she typically did to fill herself. She told me about giving herself a pat on the back and doing something nice for herself. "But I feel so guilty taking time for myself," she moped. "Do you feel guilty taking your car to the gas station when the tank is empty?" I asked.

Since that conversation I've watched for ways we women empty and fill up. I've wanted to know whether we allow ourselves to slip into depressions because of habits or attitudes or thought patterns of self-pity. I've wondered about traps vulnerable women fall into who expect everything to be perfect. I've tried to analyze what effect the past and tradition have on right now. I've talked with other women who don't have nearly as many things going for them as my lamenting friend yet seem to be bouyant, in charge, and excited about life.

I believe a woman's self-esteem level is critical to her

ability to adapt, regroup, cope, and change. I believe that if anyone out there is going to build a woman's self-esteem, it will have to be each woman herself. We could each make a list of things to help fill us when we feel empty, and although each list would vary in some specifics, all would be quite similar in many ways—pray, read, exercise, call someone, watch TV, eat, listen to the radio, go shopping, take a nap or a bath, work, clean, participate in a hobby, give service. I've tried them all. I want to get out of the mode of filling up only to empty again, and I want to fill up when I'm nine-tenths full, not when I'm below empty.

This book brings to the surface behavior patterns which empty women and suggests ways to replenish by examining thoughts, attitudes, actions, habits, and traditions which contribute to either depletion or fulfillment.

1

Where Does a Woman Fill Up?

One day Margarita, our foreign exchange student from Spain, came downstairs to find me at the computer again.

"What do you do here so long?" she asked in her sweet accent.

"Oh, I'm just doing a little writing."

"Do you mind if I ask what kind of writing?"

"I'm trying to write a chapter for a book," I answered.

"Oh, that's wonderful!" she smiled. "In Spain we say a woman is . . . how shall I say"—she ran for her Spanish-English dictionary—"fulfilled when she has given birth, planted a tree, and written a book." She paused. "Have you planted a tree?" When I told her I had, she was thrilled. Her American mom was, according to the Spanish saying, fulfilled!

She couldn't have guessed I was writing about how women can feel fulfilled. I like the simplicity of the saying she shared with me, because giving birth is the easy part of being a mother; likewise, planting a tree doesn't require nur-turing or bearing fruit; and writing a book is far easier than getting it published. I wish accomplishing those three or any other three things could permanently fill. Then if something unfulfilling (emptying) happened, I could simply say to myself, "I have given birth, planted a tree, and written a book. This unfulfilling event (or moment or thing) can't affect me, because I am filled."

Where does a woman fill up—at home, at work, at church; within or without herself? When does she fill up—in the past, present, future; when she's a wife, a mother, a single? What is it that fills spiritually, emotionally, intellectually? Are there filling stations for her? If so, are they self-serve, or is someone there to help fill her up? Who? How much does it cost? Is it possible for a woman to continually fill herself? What happens if she doesn't bother to fill up and runs on empty? Is there a word to fill in the blank in the following statement? Fuel is to an automobile as _____ is to a woman.

I've discovered that being fulfilled has little to do with being a wife or a mother. It has much more to do with being a person. Positive thoughts and attitudes, actions in tune with those thoughts and attitudes, productive habits, celebra-tions, and spirituality fill. Things which may contribute to feeling used up and empty are fatigue, ingratitude, criticism, competition, change, being sandwiched, and dependence. Are there analogies in addition to the one of filling a car with gas that help bring this issue into focus? Another one came to mind through an experience I had last year with another essential part of a car.

Help! My Battery Needs Charging

Our fourteen-year-old, John, made a final round of the University of Utah's Summer Arts Piano Competition. He was to play at noon at Snowbird, a ski resort about thirty minutes from our home. At eleven o'clock we were ready to go. We got in the car, and discovered that the battery was dead. I called a neighbor who was a retired mechanic. He came quickly with his jumper cables, but was unable to start the engine. Finally, he took the battery out of his car and put it in mine.

When we returned home, we found that our Good-Samaritan neighbor had tried unsuccessfully to charge our battery. Now he had a new one for us. He showed me a little window on the battery that looked green when the battery was charging and black if it needed charging. I thought about being filled up and being charged up. It would be nice if each of us had a gauge that would help us know when another needed a charge, when we were charged up enough to give another a boost, and when we were low ourselves. What can a woman do to be filled? Have a full tank and a charged battery. But what does that mean?

In 1969 I was teaching English at Skyline High School in Salt Lake City. I was twenty-five, married, the mother of two children, and five feet three inches tall. One afternoon the assistant principal came into my room looking for a student. I was in front of the class giving a review for a test. He looked at me and said, "Who's in charge here? Where is your teacher?" The class enjoyed the surprised look on his face when they all told him I was their teacher. He told me I should grow taller and older so he wouldn't make that mistake again. As the years have passed I have not grown taller, but I am certainly much older. No one would mistake me for a student now, but the assistant principal's words have come back to me many times as I've asked myself, "Who is in charge here?" Does being in charge boost us as a charged battery would a car?

At times I feel wonderfully in charge, as if I've been plugged into some power socket that revitalizes me inside so that I am "power-full" and energetically able to accomplish much. Other times I feel in charge of no one and nothing—especially not myself. I think, at such times, that I could slip into oblivion and no one would know the difference until the refrigerator was empty and the dishes and laundry piled up. There are even times when I feel that events have taken over and pulled the plug on whatever ability I once had to be charged up or in charge. I suspect that nobody is totally charged up (ready to act) or always in charge (taking positive action). We sometimes, of necessity, must roll with the punches. But we can take charge of which way we roll, how long we stay down, and how often we get back up. There are techniques we can learn to help us know what to do to feel in charge and charged up.

Having a dead battery or an empty gas tank are inconveniences in a car, but their equivalents in a woman may have disastrous consequences. What can I do to recharge after a financial reverse? What can I do to take charge when sickness comes to stay? If death stops close by, can I generate the energy to carry on and fill up? What can I do when I feel empty for no obvious reason? Wouldn't it be nice if we could carry an extra battery in case a transplant were needed?

Meanwhile, Back at Snowbird

During the hour John and I waited for the results of the contest, I had time to think through the events of the morning. I was thankful to have been on the receiving end of an act of service and to have arrived in time for John to compete, although the dead battery was just one of many complicating, annoying things yet to come. After we arrived at Snowbird we found a practice room; it was occupied. John sat down on a chair to wait. The chair had someone's drink from last night spilled on it, and the seat of his pants got wet. We hurried outside to see if the breeze would dry his pants. Then we saw that the practice room was available. He had been practicing for about sixty seconds when his teacher ran in to tell us we were in the wrong building, and John was scheduled to perform in five minutes! We ran to the other building. We rushed him into another practice room. One judge called for him. We went into the competition room. The other judge said they were not ready and sent us out. Then they called us back in. John sat down at the piano and played about half of his first piece. The phone in the competition room began to ring. It rang and rang—ten times. Finally one of the judges got up, answered it, and talked the whole time while John was finishing his three pieces.

So even with a charged battery and a full tank, things can go wrong!

But everything in life doesn't have to go right in order for a person to have a feeling of fulfillment.

As we proceed to think through when, where, and how a woman gets filled up and charged up, I hope we discover that we are surrounded by all the resources needed. I suspect that in most cases what I need to feel fulfilled is easily within my reach. I just need to discover what to reach for, and when and how to reach it.

Starting with the End in Mind

Every year I experience some depression around the end of August. The summer demands more, physically and emotionally, than the school year. I love having the children at home, but I get tired. On one of these last-of-summer days I had been in the car from 6:30 a.m. to 7:30 p.m. I had one last errand for the day—to pick up Dan from soccer practice. I drove to the field to find out I had arrived thirty minutes early. My frustration level was high. What was I to do with thirty more minutes in the car? But then a little voice seemed to say, "Aw, come on. Enjoy the moment."

I looked around to see if there was anything to enjoy—I

doubted there was. It was a familiar sight. The coach had divided the boys into teams—skins and shirts. They were playing a game on half the field, with only one goal and one goalie. I had seen it all many times. But then I noticed Craig, the coach, who was about twenty-seven, recently married, around six foot four, and probably 250 pounds. My attention focused on an animated Craig. He slapped his thighs and yelled, "Great block, Cory!" He jumped up and spun around in an aerial three-sixty as a goal was scored. He gleefully asked, "Hey, Dave, where were you when we needed a goal on Saturday?" Craig hugged his wife as Colin, the goalie, like a horizontal arrow, blocked a goal. "What a save, Colin! What a save!" He laughed, danced, jumped, ran, complimented, smiled, cajoled. He was completely alive in this moment in time.

In the few minutes I watched Craig, he laughed more than I had in the whole year. He was filled. He was charged up and in charge. His passion for life was contagious. I saw the boys responding, laughing, high-fiving, playing soccer with energy and skill—pleasing Craig and themselves. Then I looked beyond the field where these few boys were practicing soccer. I saw thick, green lawn, a school, children playing, houses, mountains, the sun saying farewell to the day. I saw the night coming and the stars beginning their job of giving light to the night. I saw myself suddenly happy, content, blessed to be alive and part of an orderly, splendid world.

I bowed by head and tears dropped to my shirt. I gave thanks.

Another day, months later, I was visiting an East Coast city. I had seriously begun my search for what fills us up. It was Sunday and we went to church to feel the Spirit. The congregation was a grand mix of all races and experience levels in the Church. In Relief Society the opening prayer was said by a dainty black sister in her early seventies. She had been baptized four months earlier. She stood and prayed,

"Good morning, Heavenly Father. I don't think I've said that to you yet today." Could she feel that close to and comfortable with her God and Eternal Father and not feel fulfilled? Sharing this intimate moment with this sister refreshed me. She probably greets the Father in the afternoon and evening as well.

An eighty-six-year-old widow, who weighs about as many pounds as she has years, told me about a Sunday she went to see a granddaughter confirmed and afterwards got lost in the unfamiliar ward building. "As I was trying to find my way out I saw some teenagers being very irreverent in one of the rooms. I stepped in and told them they should be quiet in the Lord's house. The shock of having a strange old lady talk to them sternly did quiet them. Just then a man rushed in, looked at me, and exclaimed, 'Oh, good! You got here. Thanks for taking the class today.' I had no idea what ward I was in or who he thought I was, but it seemed that the only proper thing to do was to teach the class!" The man who looked in her classroom, unlike the assistant principal who looked in mine, had no need to ask, "Who's in charge here?"

This is my purpose in writing—to find those experiences, opportunities, and role models that will fill, charge, expand, lift, impassion, and enrich. Thanks for coming with me. Let's begin the journey.

2

Refueling Thoughts

A penny for your thoughts is a phrase my husband uses when I seem preoccupied. Often I reply that it would be a waste of money. Yet, thoughts can be fulfilling—a creative idea, a mental image of what we may become, a memory of a precious moment in time, an impression that God is pleased with us. What can refuel or recharge us more than thoughts such as these? Thoughts are private routes leading anywhere we choose, from the debasing to the ennobling. Thoughts precede attitudes, which precede actions. What we think, we become.

If a thought-deciphering machine which printed out a person's ideas, expectations, worries, hopes, beliefs, and fears and then categorized them were hooked up to my brain for a day, what percentage of my thoughts would be under the heading "Miscellaneous, Random, and Rambling"? How many hours of thoughts would be categorized as good, bad, positive, negative, encouraging, destructive, philosophical, religious, or petty and gossipy? Should one of the answers to the question, "What can a woman do to fill up?" be to improve her thought patterns? What can we do to make our thoughts worth millions of pennies?

Life Is Difficult

M. Scott Peck begins the first chapter of his book *The Road Less Traveled* with the statement, "Life is difficult" (New York: Simon and Schuster, Touchstone Books, 1978, p. 15). When I was young I did not expect life to be hard. I thought if I did everything right, nothing would go wrong. I thought I was in control. Being in charge was natural. But the older I get the more I realize that life is difficult for 99.9 percent of us. Life is challenging, unfair, and often frustratingly full of hard work, worry, fatigue, stress, disappointment, loss, injury, pain, disease, and death. I think that when we stop expecting life to be easy, we take a giant step forward. We may not be able to control the events around us as we would like, but we can control what we think about those events and about ourselves.

As we assume more and more responsibility and are concerned about more and more people, the complexities of life mushroom. At first I was just a child, a daughter, a sister, a granddaughter. Then I became a wife. Soon I was a wife and the mother of an infant. Then I was a wife, the mother of a toddler, and the mother of another infant, and so on. I am now a wife, a mother-in-law, a grandmother, the mother of three college students, two high school students, one junior high school student, plus one elementary school student. I am a community worker and a church worker. I have been an employee. A woman may have other roles, such as divorcée, widow, student, and employer. All of these responsibilities increase the probability that the hazards of life will catch up with us.

So expecting life to be difficult, but being grateful for every minute it isn't, is a healthy thought. If we expect highs and lows, seasons and cycles, blue days, maybe even a few black days along the way, we will be better able to cope. We will be able to think, "No matter how unpleasant this moment is, it won't last forever."

Failure and Success

When things don't go right, when we fail or let an opportunity pass, when we do or say something less than perfect, we may think, "I am a failure." But failing doesn't make a person a failure. Failing means that we have discovered one way something won't work. If we think of ourselves as failures, we are—in our own minds. Failing can be a firm stepping stone. If nine out of ten things fail, then we must have the courage to try ten times as many things.

Discovering one way something won't work makes the path to success a little closer. One evening I was reading a chapter on failure in Arthur Gordon's *A Touch of Wonder*. T. J. Watson, a former president of IBM, told Gordon to analyze each failure, because those failures point the way to success. He suggested that Gordon double his failures in order to double his successes. I finished the chapter and put the book down on my dresser. As I did so I noticed a chain necklace lying on my dresser. I saw success at one end of the necklace and failure at the other. If the many inches and many more links of a chain represent steps from failure toward success, the outlook is overwhelming. How far apart success and failure seem! But then I picked up the end I had labeled failure and the other end I had called success and fastened them together around my neck. When we think of failure as discovery, we keep trying and success results.

I once heard another anecdote about Thomas Watson and failure. According to the story, he had an employee who made a ten-million-dollar mistake. The employee knew he was finished at IBM, so he wrote his resignation letter and took it to Watson. Watson looked at the letter and then at the employee and said, "Do you think I would let you leave now, after I've spent ten million dollars training you?" Appreciating failure as a teacher helps link it to success. Thinking of failure in this way is a recharging thought.

Dreams Come True

One day I had a house full of sick children, a sink full of dirty dishes, a clogged drain, and a checkbook with no money. I didn't even try to resist the thoughts of complaint that came. But then, in the back of my mind, a gnawing voice asked, "Isn't this a fulfillment of your dreams?" Like most little girls I was anxious for the day I'd be a mommy. I wanted babies by the dozens. The idea of husband, home, and children seemed like *the* answer to my fondest hopes. Often our dreams come true. But somehow, in the realization of dreams—when the dream becomes changing real dirty diapers—the similarity to the original dream is hazy. In dreams we don't realize what the dream costs, and in the accomplishment of a dream, there is often an adjustment to be made. When a dream has come true we need to acknowledge it and feel contentment rather than notice how much reality varies from the dream.

Some dreams become nightmares—marriage which ends in divorce, the ingenious business venture which turns financially sour, the desire for marriage that doesn't materialize, the dream of children unrealized because of physical problems. Yet conquer we can. The battle is in the mind. We can control our thoughts by thinking of the things we can change rather than dwelling on the things we can't. Every dream can come true if we keep hoping and dreaming, because hoping and dreaming often lead to planning and preparing, which often lead to fulfillment. Then all we have to do is make mental adjustments to compensate for the inevitable discrepancy between the dream and reality—and dream again.

Dirty-Wash Thoughts

Last spring my younger children slept at my parents' home. A few days later I went to see my mother and collect the things the children had left behind. Mother had put the forgotten items in a pile by the back door. I was ready to go when she ran into another room and came back waving a pair of socks. "Wait a minute," she called. "Are these John's?" I immediately recognized them—a pair which had defied the detergents and bleach. "Yes, thanks," I said. Embarrassed that my mother had seen such dirty socks, I quickly stuffed them into the small pocket of my parka.

On the way home I stopped at the grocery store and the dry cleaner's. I saw many people from our neighborhood. They greeted me in an unusually cheerful mannner. I thought I must somehow look special. Something was different about the way they responded to me. When I got home and hung up my parka, I saw that the dirty socks had all but made their way out of my pocket. They were hanging there for everyone to see. I knew then how funny I must have looked to everyone I met.

What is the dirty wash we sometimes hang out for others to examine? It's the negative things we express about ourselves—our idiosyncrasies, mistakes, fears, and insecurities. We take the witness stand against ourselves when we rehearse our mistakes, sins, hurts, and slights. Telling others of our follies is damaging, but this is not the worst part of hanging out the dirty wash. As we hear ourselves uttering negative things about ourselves, we not only make believers of our listeners but, more important, we reinforce negative feelings about ourselves in our own minds.

These negative statements reveal negative thoughts. We talk to ourselves in our minds all day. If this self-talk is negative ("You're indecisive," "You're forgetful," "You never were good at math," "You're fat," "Nobody appreciates you," "You are _____"), negative attitudes and actions will follow. Dirty-wash thoughts may be at the core of feeling unfulfilled. I have found that often when I talk negatively to myself I use the word *you*, as if someone else were talking to me. But when my self-talk is positive I use the word *I*. It's almost as if two voices carry on an inner conversation. "You can't." "I can." "You're failing." "I'm trying." The negative and the positive seem at war for control of thought time. The two cannot exist together. Think of the Toyota commercial in which the person is so thrilled with his new car that he leaps high into the air, his arms joyfully reaching upward. Would it be possible at such a moment to exclaim, "This is depressing!" I don't think so. If our thoughts are positive, positive actions follow. If we hang out dirty wash, negative actions follow.

Let's say I want to write a magazine article about growing amaryllis. I have my writer's guide open to the magazines that print articles of this nature. I begin to type a query letter. When I get to the end of the letter, I go to my file to get an old query so that I can copy the credits from it. As I look at that old letter I suddenly am filled with a sense of futility. There before me in the file are discarded ideas, incomplete projects, and rejection letters. I look at them and an inner voice says, "You'll never write anything worth publishing. There is no reason to finish this article. If you do you'll just add another rejection letter to the pile." But if I take control of that negative voice who thrives on dirty wash and instead say to myself, "It's worth a try," the chance for success is obvious. We often see our mistakes as headlines and our successes as fine print.

Imaging and Prayer

There is a step beyond thinking positive thoughts. My first experience with this new idea was when our youngest, Daniel, was not quite three. To compact a tedious story, Daniel had had heart surgery and seemed to be recovering. About the fourth day after the surgery, he had no appetite and was having difficulty in breathing. The doctors discovered that a lymph vessel had been cut during surgery and lymph fluid was filling his lungs. Many remedies were tried, including having Daniel eat nothing by mouth for ten days. Finally, with no promise it would solve the problem, another surgery was scheduled.

Sensing my need at this time, a friend called and explained to me the idea of imaging. She said, "In your mind, picture the surgeons working over Daniel. See in your mind the doctors looking into his heart cavity and finding the severed vessel right there in front of them. See the surgeon quickly suturing. Image the doctor coming to you and saying, 'It was so easy! Daniel will be well in a few days.' " I had little to lose. I had done the opposite for days by letting negative thoughts overwhelm and nearly consume me.

After the doctors took Daniel, I had a little cry and then decided to try imaging. I said a prayer that the operation would be successful and that I would be able to conquer the negative thoughts and image the positive. I went to the parents' waiting room to join my husband and parents. They talked and I sat, quietly creating in my mind the scene my friend had suggested. The doctors said the operation would be at least three hours long. After a half hour of my praying and imaging, the head nurse from intensive care came into the room and whispered in my ear. "I just got a call. They said Daniel will be out in about thirty minutes." "This must mean good news," I said. "I think so," she replied. After twenty minutes the surgeon came in. I knew by his gait and face that all had gone well. "We got Daniel open," he said, "and the vessel was right there in front of us, pulsing. We couldn't miss it!"

My imaging had nothing to do with the outcome of the surgery. Things don't always turn out the way we'd like. Some children do not get well. But my positive thoughts did change me. I anticipated success, and the difference this made for me was incredible. I could have sat crying and alternating between chills and sweats. I could have indulged in thinking of every possible tragic consequence, but my sanity was preserved because I filled my mind with positive images. I was in charge and thereby refueled. How powerful thoughts are!

3

Attitudes That Recharge

A new family moved into our neighborhood. Their eleven-year-old daughter came over to get acquainted with our children. She said, "Hi, my name's Katie [not her real name], and you'll get to know me real quick because I have an attitude problem."

"Why do you say that?" I asked, trying not to sound too shocked.

"Well, everyone says that to me. They always have. That's why I have to go to special classes at school."

We've become well acquainted with Katie. She is an interesting child—rather innocent. She lacks confidence and has been negatively labeled, but we like her.

One day Katie had come over to play, but no one was at home except Richard and me. She asked if I was busy. I was loading the dishes into the dishwasher. She offered to help. "No one ever lets me help," she confided. "I think they think I'll break something or mess it up."

"I'd be glad to have your help," I said.

She loaded all the plastic and the silverware, leaving the sharp knives and the glassware to me. "You're a good kid, Katie," Richard said as we finished. She smiled and left.

In a few minutes she was back. "What kind of a kid did your husband say I was?" she asked.

I had to think what she was referring to. "A good kid," I said. "You are a good helper and friend. I like you."

She came back the next day and said she wanted to tell her dad what kind of kid we'd said she was. I told her again. Is it possible that that was the first time she had been told she was a good kid? If so, it's no wonder she's been labeled as a child with an attitude problem.

Many of us have grown up not knowing that others like us or think we have worth. I have read parenting tips from the forties and fifties which caution parents about telling a child he does things well because it would make the child conceited and self-centered. We know now that just the opposite is true. We need others to tell us that we have value, that we are good at many things. But we don't have that control. We do have control, of course, over the value we place on ourselves. If no one else tells me that I'm a good kid, I must do it myself. Building a positive attitude about myself and my surroundings generates filled-up and charged-up feelings.

An Attitude Check

Is there a way to check my attitude? Am I more negative or more positive? One way to find out is to analyze first impulses and thoughts in new situations.

1. When I receive a first-ever phone call from my child's school principal, is my initial reaction
   A. Oh, no! He's in trouble; B. Oh, no! She must have

been injured; C. I'll bet he wants me to work in PTA; D. I'll bet my child has done something good.

2. When I sign a contract to buy a car, is my first thought
   A. I hope this car won't be another lemon; B. (If it's new) Now the Joneses will have to keep up with me; C. (If it's old) This pile of junk will probably fall apart at the first pothole; D. I'll probably get hit driving off the lot; E. This car is a good choice for us at this time in our lives.

3. When I do something I am not proud of, do I think
   A. Oh, well, nobody's perfect; B. It's So-and-So's fault. If he hadn't . . . ; C. I'm always doing dumb things like this; D. It was not a good choice, but I'm going to make it right and try harder next time.

Of course, the last option is the best choice in each case. It's easy to see this when the questions are in print. But in a fleeting moment of thought, how do I respond—negatively or positively, with paranoia or with courage, expecting the worst or with energy anticipating the best, realistically or impractically, selfishly or selflessly?

Satisfaction

There's a comfort zone around those who feel basically satisfied with who they are and where they are headed. Every time I complain about the weather I recall the classic poem about the nature of dissatisfied persons.

> As a rule man's a fool.
> When it's hot
> He wants it cool.
> When it's cool

He wants it hot.
Always wanting what it's not,
Never wanting what he's got.
(Author unknown.)

I've heard several versions of the following woeful tale centered on this theme that man is never satisfied.

As soon as I get in high school, I'll be happy; that is, if I learn to ski.

I wish this snow would melt. I'm so tired of the cold.

High school is so boring. As soon as I'm in college and can choose the classes I take, then I'll be happy.

I wish I had a car.

I wish I had a girlfriend.

My parents are unfair in expecting me to pay the insurance on the car. Keeping gas in it takes every cent of my allowance. I don't have money to date.

A job would solve all my problems.

Having to work after school makes me get poor grades.

Now that I'm in college everything will be perfect.

These dorms make me claustrophobic. I'll be happy in an apartment of my own.

The opposite sex is so hard to understand.

I am lonely. I want to get married.

Once I graduate I'll be content—never a complaint again.

If we could only afford a house and have a baby everything would be fine.

If only you could walk and talk.

If only you'd be quiet and listen to your parents once in a while.

We need a second car and a dishwasher.

Working nine to five, five days a week, is the pits. I miss the fun, the freedom of the college days.

When the kids are married and on their own, then I'll be happy. It will be just the two of us again. Those were the blissful days.

I miss the good ol' days when the kids were home.

This house is too big, and something always needs fixing.

Grandchildren would liven up this condo.

Don't they realize we don't want to raise our grandkids.

When was the last time the grandchildren came over?

I'll be happy when I retire.

Did you pay the last payment on the cemetery plots?

Life is so boring since I retired.

I miss the old house.

If you don't have your health . . .

Gratitude

Feeling grateful, the opposite of dissatisfied, is one way to improve attitude. If I focus on what I need, what I'm not, what I've lost, who offended me, what I might have been, or what I'm doing without, I have an attitude problem. My dissatisfaction and ingratitude show when I whine or complain or gripe or grumble or crab or bellyache. In the scriptures it's called murmuring. The question in Malachi 3:8, "Will a man rob God?" can also refer to the thanks God should receive. Will a man rob God by failing to acknowledge his hand in all things? (see D&C 59:21.)

The Lord has a way of reminding us to be thankful. If things (food, shelter, health, opportunity, life) are taken away, we become acutely aware of their absence. As a mundane illustration, my neighbor's dryer broke. It would have cost more to repair than replace. She went without one for three months. How grateful she was for a new dryer!

When my car, appliances, and body are working well, do I remember to give thanks? Do I notice the multitude of blessings or just the one inconvenience? The ratio of blessings to problems is about the same as the mote to the beam. Do I notice the small and insignificant instead of the wondrous and great? Amulek challenges us to "live in thanksgiving daily, for the many mercies and blessings which [God] doth bestow upon [us]" (Alma 34:38). An attitude of gratitude fills and charges.

Attitude Barometer

Someone else's attitude is easy to categorize. "He radiates happiness." "She's love personified." "He's the world's champion grouch." "Who spit in her Cheerios?" Such good judges we think we are of others—but that's a subject for another page. The issue here is how good a judge of ourselves we are. Do we see ourselves as others see us? Is the attitude we think we have truly the one we reflect? Here are a few categories in which to rate yourself as to attitude.

1. Do you feel that if someone else does something good, that somehow detracts from your "goodness"? This is the "If you rise, I go down" syndrome. You can catch yourself showing this attitude when in conversation you top another's story or when you feel you have to have something someone else has.

2. Do you feel with Murphy that if anything can go wrong, it will and that there is no limit to how bad things can get? You can get an idea whether you are optimistic or pessimistic by writing down what you think will go wrong today. An optimist would answer that nothing will go wrong. The longer your list, the more pessimistic you are.

3. How patient are you? Do you raise an eyebrow or the roof?

4. Do you find ways to defuse disasters instead of contributing to them? Observe yourself to see if your personality brings out the best or the worst in others.

5. Do you see life as a soap opera—barely untangling one

troublesome situation before another starts? You can rate yourself by listening to what you tell others about your life. Which do you rehearse in more detail, the good or the bad?

6. Do you treat your children and your friends with the same respect? The next time a child spills a glass of red punch would be a good time to check your attitude toward children.

7. What do you see when you look in the mirror? Do you see gentle eyes, wrinkles that give you a look as if you are always smiling, or are you only aware of the out-of-place hair, the double chin, the blemishes?

8. How do you react to criticism? Do you feel you have been hurt, so you counterhurt with your list of criticisms? Do you counterhurt with the "silent treatment"? Do you analyze the criticism and find it valid and thank the person who had the courage to tell you? After analysis, do you feel the criticism was unjust but forgive the person and go on? Do you appreciate honest feedback from others?

9. Are you self-centered or can you step outside your own needs and concerns to lift others. I like Emerson's words: "Every man takes care that his neighbor shall not cheat him, but a day comes when he begins to care that he does not cheat his neighbor. Then all goes well. He has changed his marketcart into a chariot of the sun."

10. Do you strive to expect more of yourself and less of others? Your stress level will decrease when the gap between expectation and reality decreases. Your stress over another's imperfections likely produces ulcers, not the hoped-for changes.

11. Are you appreciative of your talents—the differences that make you unique? If only the birds with the prettiest voices sang, the woods would be very quiet. An attitude of using and developing talents shows maturity.

12. Do you believe this statement? "What I gave, I have. What I spent, I had. What I kept, I lost."

13. I believe I am a child of God. But do I truly believe that you are a child of God, too? I believe Christ died for my

sins. Do I believe he died for you too? Do I admire the god-like qualities I see in you because they are evidence of the dignity of man and the divinity of God?

14. Do you help others reach their full potential? Do you catch them doing things right? Do you catch yourself doing things right?

15. Are the glasses of root beer in your life half empty or half full?

Evergreen

In business the term *evergreen* applies to a source of revenue that just keeps coming in. Interest paid on a bank account is evergreen, as are dividends, rentals, and royalties. It doesn't take continuous effort. Once the system is in place, the money flows in. A positive attitude about one's self and life in general is an evergreen. The greatest evergreen in life that I know of is the philosophy based on scripture: "Give, and it shall be given unto you; good measure, pressed down, and shaken together, and running over, shall men give into your bosom. For with the same measure that ye mete withal it shall be measured to you again" (Luke 6:38). We can give:

time—all it takes,

tolerance—judging not,

empathy—entering into another's world by walking in
    his shoes,

interest—in other's interests, and

thanks—in word and action.

All of this is giving service, which the Marriott hotels say is the ultimate luxury and which the scripture says will come back to us. The benefits cannot be calculated. It is a way to have good things flow to you without force or effort. So one answer to our question "What can a woman do to fill up?" is to have a positive attitude. Attitude determines at what altitude we fly through life.

4

Putting the Past in the Past

Many of our attitudes affect how filled up we feel. But our attitude about the past defines, probably more than any other, how we conduct our lives, because the past keeps accumulating. Every minute there's more of it either to cope with or be thankful for. Our attitude about the past determines how we feel about the future.

Along with about twenty other mothers, I attended a meeting of PTA volunteers at the PTA president's home. The PTA president's college-age daughter, Lisa, who had been conscripted by her mother to take minutes, was also there.

As women do after meetings, we began to talk, and the conversation centered on Lisa. The usual questions of "What are you majoring in?" and "How do you like living away from home?" soon changed into an if-only-I-could-be-your-age-again-I'd-sure-do-a-lot-of-things-differently confession and advice session.

"If only I'd known how much I'd want a degree, I'd have waited to get married," said one.

"Major in the highest paying field possible," advised another. "You'll never regret the ability to make a lot of money."

"Oh, I don't think that's so important," cautioned another from across the room. "Follow your heart. Do what *you* want—not what will make you the most money or what your parents advise or what your intellectual side says would be wisest. I wish every day I had become an artist. But everyone told me I'd never make any money and that there was too much competition. Unfortunately, I believed them."

"Well, whatever you do, don't rush into marriage," said another. At age twenty I thought I knew all there was to know. Have many and varied experiences before you marry. You are married for a long, long, *long* time."

"I agree," said another. "I was married at thirty-two, and that was just right."

"If only someone had said to me . . . "

"If only I had realized that . . . "

"If only I hadn't . . . "

"If only . . . if only."

Lisa probably tuned out early on, but what of this phrase "if only"? There are things in every woman's life she would change if she had the chance to, but sometimes the past is so present that we are sandwiched between today and yesterday. There are several theories as to the validity of "if only" statements. One theory says that if you could go back and live a segment of your life again, even with the advantage of hindsight, you would probably make most of the same choices. We say we would have done things differently, but being ourselves, thinking as we do, the script would have been pretty much the same. The idea has merit. We do make the same kinds of mistakes over again, even when we know better. This philosophy does not comfort us much in situations where a poor decision in hindsight looked like a choice with good potential in the beginning.

The second theory suggests that if we could live life again we would do many things differently. This theory says that of course we learn from our mistakes. Just think of any test you have ever taken. After the test was graded, if you had the opportunity to study for a week and retake it, you likely would do much better. But there is no guarantee here either. As one of the characters in Madeleine L' Engle's *The Arm of the Starfish* points out, "You cannot see the past that did not happen any more than you can foresee the future" (New York: Ariel Books, 1965, p. 220).

Robert Frost's well-known and oft-quoted poem tells of choices—of two roads diverging in a yellow wood and of a choice that made all the difference. Any road we choose has its own consequences. Just around the bend of any choice, we meet face-to-face with its consequences. But when we look at choices in hindsight, we tend only to see the benefits that would have come—not the hard work, inconvenience, sacrifice, blisters, or potential for failure. We only know the consequences of the path we took, yet sometimes in our "if only" reflections we think the other ways would have been smoother, or happier, or easier, or less fraught with this or that. But we will never know, because "way leads on to way." Every choice opens its own opportunities and eliminates others. Today, if I choose to wear a red dress, I can't wear a dress of any other color. If I make pizza for dinner, we can't have hamburgers or chicken. These opportunity eliminations seem harmless, but what about a choice such as: if I marry Bill, I can't marry Tom, Dick, or Harry.

Yet in Hindsight

I like to think my vision into the past is at least 20-20. I know just what mistakes I made; when, where, and why I made them; and what I could have and should have done differently. I think that if I could take the road test through my past a second time, I'd just zip through with no errors. My childish fears and immature choices would be easy to eliminate. Since there would be few mistakes or sins, I would not suffer many unpleasant consequences. Since mistakes and their aftermath take time, imagine how much more I would accomplish on a straight line to happiness and success! It's a science fiction lover's dream to think about where this road or that choice would have led.

At times I relive the moments preceding a poor choice and endure afresh the pain or embarrassment or failure. Poignant emotions surface again and again, taking new energy and time. In church one Sunday we discussed the topic of how to forgive and forget. Everyone agreed that the forgiving seemed easier than the forgetting. A woman who has been both a divorcée and a widow spoke of her way of forgetting. She said she could not forget segments of her life, but she could, in time, learn to eliminate the emotion she felt about the negative segments. She concluded by saying, "The past is for learning from, not living in. Put a period on yesterday. If you don't, hardening of the attitudes will happen to you."

If Only

We have talked about "if only" statements which reflect negative feelings. "If only" statements are usually followed by "but also" phrases. We could make a very detailed list of all the "if onlys" in our lives. We could also list the good, the successful, the happy, the things that bring us joy, the loyalties we feel, the things we are proud of, and even the near successes and almost noteworthy things in our lives. These I think of as the "but alsos." There are always things that go awry in life, but also there are the things that do go right. A friend, Susan, who was our Christine's fourth-grade teacher, emphasized the positive in her life and made a "but also" list. She didn't call it that, but I was so impressed with her attitude that I've saved her list these many years (Christine is now sixteen). Susan's positive attitude made her a popular and successful teacher and friend to each of her students. Here is her list:

I, Susan, am

—a native of Ajo (Garlic) Arizona
—an observer of a thousand beautiful sunsets
—a one-time state archery champion
—a transplanted "desert rat" to the cold winters of Utah
—a graduate of the great BYU
—a lover of nature
—a hiker at Mill Hollow day camp
—a patient listener of ideas
—a reader of historical novels and a few science fiction ones
—a balancer of home and work
—a devout eater of good Mexican food
—a continuous student
—an anxious, indulgent mother of four sons
—an honored, outstanding thespian
—the owner of season tickets to the University of Utah theatre
—the wife of Gary, psychologist and part-time student
—the president of a young women's organization
—a part-time painter, paperhanger, and general remodeler
—a collector of unfinished projects
—the owner of twelve chickens
—a player of table games
—and an elementary school teacher who loves her work!

Susan's past is a friend, not an ever-present foe. Her "but also" statements are self-fulfilling prophecies. She seems to be saying that she gains courage and enthusiasm for life as she builds on those elements of her life that are positive. Being the owner of twelve chickens does not make headlines, but it, along with the other items on her list, gives her and us a feeling of a complete personality, a healthy human being. Her attitude gives her a filled-up feeling.

The Past Trap

I have another friend who constantly battles the "if onlys" of the past, and this causes her to fly at a low altitude. When I noticed that she was caught in a "past trap," I wrote her a letter to say certain things better than I could face-to-face.

Dear Friend,
    When we talked last night, I sensed that your past is bothering you. I hope you don't feel I am overstepping the bounds of our friendship in writing you this letter. We have all made mistakes and committed sins, and I am absolutely sure I haven't made my last mistake or committed my last sin.
    None of the things you worry about has caused others to permanently suffer. Your family doesn't suffer now because of the concern they had for you then. The opposite is true. Their rejoicing over you is nearly complete. The "nearly" will be erased when you forgive yourself. Changing your attitude about the past can help you take charge of the present. With the proper attitude, mistakes we make and sins we commit can make us stronger and more disciplined in choosing the right.
    I've heard of trappers who go into the jungles to trap monkeys for zoos. The trappers have observed the monkeys and discovered a trait which makes them easy to

catch. Metal boxes are chained to the jungle trees. Inside are the monkeys' favorite nuts. A small hole is cut in the top of the box, just the right size for a little monkey's hand to slip through. The trappers leave. Soon a monkey discovers something new in the jungle. He shakes the box. He sees and smells the nuts. He puts his hand inside and gathers a fistful of nuts. Suddenly his joy is frustrated as he discovers that with a fistful of nuts his hand can't get through the hole in the box. Instead of letting go of the nuts and being free, the monkey will stand, fist wrapped tightly around the nuts, until the trappers come and take him away. The monkey traps himself.

Sometimes we do the same thing. We keep our fists tightly clenched around incidents in the past and are caught in a past trap—a trap that we can be free of if we will only emotionally let go of such incidents. If we can free ourselves of the negative emotions and be forever grateful for the lessons learned, we can go forward as never before. I know I will not make some mistakes now, because I learned the hard way then. I think this is good. I am more aware of so many good things now. I shudder at the thought of some of my mistakes, and I teach others to avoid such actions with an intensity I could not otherwise feel. I don't mean to excuse sin or suggest that anyone try it just to know how awful it is.

Others have long since forgiven you. I'm sure the Lord has forgiven you. Now forgive yourself. Let the past be in the past. Jesus already atoned for your sins. The reward of righteous living is peace. Claim that blessing. Instead of looking back with regret, look forward with thanks.

To Recharge

In 1 Corinthians we read about faith, hope, and charity. Paul says, "The greatest of these is charity." But when we are in the attitude-recharging business, hope is the greatest. When there seems to be nothing else, there still can be hope. No matter what has happened in our past—ten minutes ago, yesterday, or ten years ago—we can go forward today, right now, if we have hope.

President Ezra Taft Benson has said: "We live in an age when, as the Lord foretold, men's hearts are failing them, not only physically but in spirit (see D&C 45:26). Many are giving up heart for the battle of life. . . . As the showdown between good and evil approaches with its accompanying trials and tribulations, Satan is increasingly striving to overcome the Saints with despair, discouragement, despondency, and depression.

"Yet, of all people, we as Latter-day Saints should be the most optimistic and the least pessimistic." ("Do Not Despair," in *Hope* [Salt Lake City: Deseret Book Co., 1988], p. 1.)

Elder John H. Groberg made this statement about hope: "No matter what price we have to pay, or how long we must suffer, there is always hope. No matter how deep the wound, how dark the night, keep up hope. It is worth it. There is always hope!" ("There Is Always Hope," in *Hope*, p. 65.)

Hope charges a battery and fills a tank. Today, I will show my hopeful attitude by writing a "but also" list.

5

Actions That Fill

Thinking and imaging are private matters. Attitudes and feelings are quite personal but can be sensed by others. Actions are more public. Others judge us by our actions and then make assumptions as to what feelings and thoughts preceded the actions. We judge our own actions more harshly than our thoughts or attitudes because it's more difficult to change a regrettable action. Certain actions empty; others fill our tank with positive thoughts and feelings about ourselves. Feeling good—having a full tank and a charged battery—is directly proportional to the number of positive actions we see ourselves perform. A positive action may be as simple as smiling at a child in the grocery store or as complicated as loving and helping a wayward stepchild every day.

Set Realistic Goals

The times when I feel most out of control are those

hours, days, weeks, even months or years when I feel stagnated. The times when I feel most in control are times when I have goals and am moving towards achieving them. For me, feelings of being filled up and charged up mean I have set small, realistic, easily attainable goals which provide opportunity for frequent success. Major and long-term, even lifetime, goals provide basic direction to life, but to achieve them many minigoals must be reached along the way. I have set some giant goals, which usually begin with the words *always* and *never.* "Never get angry." "Always be sensitive to others' needs." These goals usually remain unachieved because *always* and *never* are such long time periods. Discouragement rather than confidence results. If I set the goal never to raise my voice again, I can predict I will fail. But if I set a goal that today I will not raise my voice before ten in the morning, I can succeed. Then when ten o'clock comes and I have not raised my voice, what do I do? Set another goal? Not yet. First I give myself a pat on the back. We do this for others. We praise and compliment them. We even create situations for our children to have guaranteed success. Usually no one creates such opportunities for us. We have to do it for ourselves. A pat on the back and a compliment are encouraging, even if they are from me to me. As we keep the cycle in motion—set a minigoal, feel good about the achievement, set another minigoal—we are recharged.

I have learned from my husband an important principle about feeling good about myself. When he accomplishes something (let's say he has just mowed the lawn), he enjoys the success. When I accomplish something, I tend to see the imperfections in my work. I think about how much better someone else could have done it or how much better I should have done it. But not Richard. He will go to the back window and look out at the newly mowed lawn three or four times during the day. He never says a word, but I can tell from the look on his face that he is saying to himself, "You did a good job; the lawn looks great."

Show Respect

Another action we can do to be more in charge is to show respect to family, relatives, friends, peers, children, strangers, and ideas. We usually do this—999,999 times out of a million. Well, maybe that's too idealistic. How about ninety-nine times out of a hundred? Anyway, it's that one time when temper flares and we lose control that we remember forever. (The person who is the object of our anger probably never forgets either.)

When I was sixteen I worked at the candy counter at the JC Penney store in Sugarhouse, an area in Salt Lake City. The candy counter was four-sided, which made it tricky to keep track of who came before whom. (The system of taking numbers wasn't in use then.) One morning I was cleaning out the candy bins because there were no customers. Finally a woman came and stood in front of me and asked for some candy. The kind she wanted was right where I was working. I put the scoop into the bin and then I heard a voice from behind me say, "You can't treat me like that." I assumed that the woman who spoke these words must have been waiting, so I began to apologize. She did not want to be appeased and continued her tirade. Her voice became louder and louder and her words more and more angry. She ended by saying I could not insult her that way and get away with it. She was going to report me to the manager, which she did. It was a traumatic experience for me, and the picture of her angry face always stayed in the back of my mind. The manager later told me her name, so I had a name and a face to remember.

Six years later, as newlyweds, Richard and I moved into an apartment in Sugarhouse. It was not many days before I discovered that this woman was our neighbor. Neither she nor I ever mentioned the incident that occurred six years earlier, but I knew she remembered me as I remembered her, because she bathed me in kindness. It was her way of apologizing. But I hadn't been harmed by the incident. She was the one who had carried a burden of guilt for six years. She knew she had let her temper lash out at a young girl selling candy in Penney's. As we show respect to others we say to ourselves: "I treat others with respect; therefore, I am a respectable person," and saying this recharges us.

Listen

I have seen the phrase "active listening" in parenting and education books. We encourage others to talk when we actively listen—when our eyes meet theirs and when we make appropriate comments. Active listeners don't wait for a pause in conversation so they can tell you something about themselves. They are interested in you and in what you are saying. It is possible, however, to fake active listening. Fake listeners look as if they are listening and respond as if they are listening, but their minds and emotions are someplace else. You can test yourself to find out if you are an active listener. Next time someone is rambling on and on, and you feel that you'd like to cut the conversation short, imagine that you are in a courtroom and have to repeat this conversation for the judge. An active listener is part of even a seemingly one-way conversation as she encourages more conversation by using appropriately spaced phrases: "Oh, really!" "Is that right?" "How interesting!"

One of our children had a teacher I met for the first time at parent/teacher conference. I liked her immediately. She made me feel important. I felt she cared about my child. I felt I had gained a helper in raising my child. When I got home and was thinking about what had made me like this woman so much so quickly, I realized that I liked her because she was fully present. She listened intently with her whole person.

But listening is hard. Listening takes time. Listening takes concentration. Listening takes control. As I work on being fully present in conversation, I find that active listening is a recharging experience for both listener and speaker. The listener is focused, respectful, empathetic, encouraging, interested, but not nosey. The speaker is heard, respected, encouraged, and given the chance to express feelings. Both listener and speaker keep confidences; both use reinforcing phrases and words—never turnoffs or put-downs. Both are involved in and gain from the experience of listening, because the speaker is listening to herself too.

A few weeks after the parent/teacher conference, I saw a friend who told me of a friend of hers whose baby had died minutes after birth. She told me of a wonderful woman who was helping this friend deal with the loss. The woman headed an organization that helps mothers whose babies die shortly after birth. My friend learned that for the past fifteen years this woman had personally called every mother in their community whose baby had died. She would listen to the mothers and assess what her organization could do to help. This woman started the organization and does all the initial calling, because her first baby had died at birth and there was no support group then. My friend happened to mention the name of this wonderful woman. Yes, it was my child's teacher. She had paid a high price to make listening an action that fills and recharges herself and others.

Volunteer

I have always felt that I have too much to do to volunteer for anything additional. In committee meetings I sit back hoping all the assignments will be taken by others. The recent influence of a neighbor has changed my mind about the power in volunteering.

I first became acquainted with Ann when she came to collect for the cancer drive. We met again when she came collecting for the heart association. This time I noticed she was limping. "Oh, just a little skiing accident. I'm getting better every day." I learned that she teaches school and is a leader in her church. When a group of the neighborhood mothers decided to have an "Olympics" for the neighborhood children, I asked Ann if she had any time to make a few phone calls. "I'd love to. Thanks for asking," she replied. Well, she not only made many phone calls, she also had one of the events in her yard, was the unofficial photographer for the event, had prints of the photos made, at her expense, for each child, lent us her whistle and clipboards, made brownies for the children's sack lunches, and offered to pay for the drinks.

A few months later I met Ann at the first PTA meeting of the year. The school needed volunteer lay readers. Again it was the same excitement. "I'm going to be a lay reader. It sounds like so much fun! I can buy stickers and write encouraging notes on each child's paper. It will be great!" I noticed she was still limping.

There are many charities, such as the PTA, that are run entirely by volunteers. But to have the benefits of volunteering you don't have to work in the PTA or at the hospital or home-less shelter or go door to door to collect for one of the seemingly endless good causes. You can volunteer in your own home. When a child needs help with a school report, when he breaks a plate and is having trouble getting all the pieces picked up, when your hubby is in the bathroom and needs something brought to him, you can volunteer to help. Phrases such as "Here, I'll help," "I can do that for you," "I'll run outside and get it," "I'd be glad to" bring a gentle spirit into a home and also teach the principles of respect, kindness, and volunteering.

If we are assigned to do something, we do it because we are assigned. It becomes duty. We are not in charge of the assign-ment. But if we volunteer, we have chosen to become involved. We are in charge.

Kindness

I once heard the story of a woman who decided to be perfect for just one day. As things inevitably started to go wrong, she found perfection wasn't possible, because the world is full of imperfect people. She became discouraged. A few months later she decided to try being not perfect but kind for a day. As the inevitable again began to test her goal, she found much to her delight that in spite of the things she couldn't control, she still could be kind. At the end of the day she wrote in her journal, "I succeeded in being kind all day and, surprising as it sounds, I was nearly perfect." Affirmative action creates an in-charge feeling. It's a two-sided blessing. Both giver and receiver are enriched.

One of the women I visit teach taught me about kind actions which recharge. The month had slipped by, and I hadn't been to see her. It was the evening of the twenty-ninth when she knocked at my door. There she stood with three newly bottled jars of fruit—one of peaches, one of pears, and one of cherries. She said, "We're just leaving to go out of town for a few days. I knew you would want to get your visiting teaching done, so count it done in reverse." I feel loved and cared for every time I think of her kindness, and I'm sure it recharged her as well.

An article in the *Church News* stated that the Relief Society was beginning the commemoration of its 150th year. The general presidency suggested a way to celebrate. They asked each sister to do one charitable act each day. We likely do many such acts already each day, but if we all do at least one, how many millions of lives will be touched! And then let's assume that each good deed inspires another good deed, and then another and another. The ripple effect of one kindness after another cannot go unnoticed. The world will be a better place because of our actions that fill ourselves and others.

6

Habits That Recharge

I have some habits I'd like to break, but this is easier said than done. Habits are fixed response patterns. I would like to think my unproductive and self-defeating habits are inborn, involuntary, but I understand that all habits are learned. If an action which required awareness at first is repeated often enough, that action becomes part of us—almost instinctive or automatic, requiring little or no thought. For this reason, self-defeating habits can continue after the reason for the habit is gone. The story of Panquito, the little donkey, illustrates this idea.

The Little Donkey

Every day Panquito carried salt from the mine to the village. As he plodded along toward the market, he had to cross a stream. His master, a boy named Jorge, had to encourage

Panquito forward nearly every step of the journey to market, especially through the stream. One day as Jorge was pushing the little donkey through the stream, Panquito lost his footing and slipped on a rock. He disliked the cold water, but as he got up out of the stream, he realized that his load was suddenly lighter. For many days Panquito "slipped" again and again into the stream. The naughty donkey was losing much money for Jorge, because when they did get to market, the salt that wasn't dissolved in the stream was wet and unsalable. But Jorge's anger and threats did nothing to convince Panquito to cease his undesirable behavior.

An older friend suggested to Jorge that he change his product. "Make arrangements with the man who collects sponges," he suggested. "Panquito will carry sponges easily because they are so much lighter than salt." The agreement was made, and Jorge loaded Panquito with the sponges. The load was light, lighter than anything Panquito had ever experienced, but he had a self-defeating habit. As they crossed the stream, he "slipped," half drowning. He struggled to make his way out of the water. His self-defeating habit had increased his burden manyfold as the sponges suddenly became even heavier than the salt.

Discovering Self-defeating Habits

We probably all carry some soggy sponges. Usually no one stops us and says, "Pardon me, it's probably none of my business, but do you realize that you are carrying the extra burden of an unproductive habit?" We need to examine our thoughts, attitudes, and actions to discover our own self-defeating habits. The first step in changing an unproductive habit (such as slipping into the stream when a burden seems too heavy) is to be aware the habit exists. We are acutely aware of some of our bad habits. We make lists and New Year's resolutions to improve in those areas. But other habits aren't as easy to work on, because we don't consider certain actions as self-defeating habits. Often a bad habit is totally obvious to everyone but the owner of the habit. Discovering unproductive habits may be difficult and unpleasant. We can discover self-defeating habits by taking note of others' negative responses to us. Such responses often come in answer to negative habits in us. We can then deduce backwards to discover what the habit is. This method is only moderately accurate, because so much guessing and assuming are involved. A more direct method is to ask someone we trust to make us aware of our bad habits. (One at a time, please.) Before using this method, we must make sure we are prepared for the answers. We cannot become defensive. If we open ourselves up for criticism, we need the courage to accept it and act on it. Some bad habits are merely annoyances; others turn out to be the sum of character, our innermost core, and greatly affect how in charge or uncharged we feel.

For example, if I am told I have a phony-sounding laugh, a high-pitched and irritating voice, a funny wave, or a mousy handshake, or if I am told I am a chronic complainer or put people down in conversation, can I take the criticism and change my behavior? If I am told I procrastinate, am late with assignments, or use poor grammar, am I willing to do better? If I am told I gossip, exaggerate, lie, or lack sensitivity, how will I adjust?

Kicking the Habit

Once I come to the knowledge of my bad habit, the next step is even more challenging. Now I am aware of a self-defeating habit; yes, I want to change, but how do I do it? Here are five possible methods:

1. *Cold Turkey.* Just quit, right this minute, and never repeat the habit again. There are situations in which the consequences of a habit hit so hard that we shudder and

whisper to ourselves, "From this moment on, from this time forward, I will never do that again." This takes discipline, discipline, discipline. But if a habit can be eliminated this way, why not?

2. *Substitution.* In eliminating a bad habit we may create an empty space—a vacuum which begs to be filled. The substitution method of kicking a habit can help. To change a habit by substitution or replacement, create a new habit—a beneficial one. Catch yourself as you are about to engage in the old habit, and put the new one in its place. I have heard of smokers who quit by chewing gum or other substances. I have heard of people who want to eliminate a swear word from their vocabularies, so they substitute another word in place of the offensive one. The habit of watching too much TV can be lessened by planning alternate activities to do during the usual TV time. As a child I was taught that to change a habit it must be avoided twenty-one consecutive times. Sounds simple, but focus, purpose, and determination in big doses are needed. As you attempt to change a habit, complications may result because old habits are so comfortable. If you chew gum to quit smoking, you may end up with both habits.

3. *Reward/Punishment.* Some people are most successful when rewards and/or punishments are attached to goals. If I lose twenty-five pounds, I will get ___ . If I don't criticize anyone today, I will get ___ . If I don't procrastinate once today, I will get ___ . If I do overeat today, my punishment will be ___ . If I do exaggerate today, my punishment will be ___ . Although this method is more complex and takes more thought time, it works! Keep in mind that rewards usually work better than punishments.

4. *Visualization.* Visualization is another word for imaging. If I can visualize myself as being free of self-defeating habit, I will see that I will like myself better. I can, for a few moments in my brain, feel what it will feel like to be free of

the habit. I can see what I will be like without the habit. I will want the benefits of being free of that unproductive habit. Through this visualization I will receive motivation to discard my self-defeating habit. Visualize yourself acting, not reacting, the next time you feel angry. Visualize yourself feeling in charge next time you lack confidence. See yourself calming yourself next time you feel stressed or anxious. William Arthur Ward's beautiful axiom is true. "If you can imagine it, you can achieve it. If you can dream it, you can become it."

5. *Time*. Time is a secret weapon. It can work wonders on unwanted habits. A habit is often a response mechanism. It may be a cover-up technique for an insecurity. It may be a counterhurt response. If we can condition ourselves to place time between the provocation and our reaction, more productive responses will usually be the result. The idea of counting to ten is a method of using time. Yet, this is what may happen: "One." *Oh! I am so angry!* "Two." *How could any thinking person allow this to happen?* "Three." *What on earth am I to do?* "Four." *I am mad, mad, mad!* "Five." Yell. "Six." Slam something down and stamp foot. And so on. This habit of counting to ten at least delays a negative reaction and subdues it. But a higher level of using time may create a higher habit.

Counting to ten can be done nearly unconsciously. What would happen if next time I'm provoked I immediately put something positive, something which takes conscious thought, in my mind? This positive thought would not only place some time between anger and response but also divert my attention to something positive. There are two diversions I find helpful. The first is using a song to fill the gap. I choose one to fit the mood. The second method is to take a video of positive memories out of the library in my mind and play it for a few seconds—until I feel in charge of the situation.

All habits are learned. All habits can be unlearned. To

accomplish this, bring an unwanted habit to the level of awareness. Catch yourself in the act and intervene by quitting cold turkey, substituting a better habit, using rewards or punishments, visualizing yourself without the habit, utilizing time by humming your favorite tune or by playing one of your favorite mental videos as a temporary distraction.

Why Change Self-Defeating Habits?

Is the only reason to change a self-defeating habit the charge we feel as we accomplish our goal? There may be a more compelling reason. Habits seem to be hereditary. Several generations may have a certain character trait or vice because of someone else's habit.

Traditions may be thought of as group habits. I know of a boy who wanted to join a prestigious club but decided against it because he had heard that the older boys in the club had a tradition of initiating new members. The initiations involved something painful and humiliating. Nevertheless, the boy was finally persuaded to join. The first weekly meeting came and sure enough, after the adults had gone, the older boys had a surprise waiting for the new boy. He bore the indignities well and afterwards announced to the boys, "I think this is a gross way to treat someone. I will never let you initiate other new guys. This tradition stops with me!"

I grew up with the most patient mother in the world. I can never remember hearing her raise her voice. When I thank her for the habit she has given me of patience and long-suffering, she says something like, "Well, I had that same example in my home. I grew up with it. I didn't know there was any other way to be." Our responsibility is to pass on the good habits our ancestors have given to us and to conquer any self-defeating habits so they will not be inflicted upon another generation.

Future Generations

Thoughts of my posterity motivate me to want to change an unproductive habit. When I see in my mind future grandchildren or great-grandchildren being burdened by a habit that I could have but did not correct, I feel as if I'm having a nightmare. I worry that even little bad habits may become big bad habits in the future. What if in frustrating or angry moments I were to use name-calling as a way to express frustration. Think of generations after me calling their children and their children's children names because of my habit. I want to replace the habit of name-calling with a habit that frees my posterity from that tradition. I want to use words that build a person rather than tear him down or label him. One of the most recharging habits we can cultivate is use of the three hardest phrases to say: "I'm sorry," "I was wrong," and "I love you." Frustrations melt when you simply say, "You're right." No defensive melodrama, no justifications, no blaming others. I hope to gain the habit of using these most important phrases of the English language often so that my posterity will. Proverbs 17:28 suggests the same. "Even a fool, when he holdeth his peace, is counted wise: and he that shutteth his lips is esteemed a man of understanding."

The other habit I'd like not to pass on to my posterity is the habit of procrastinating. "The roof doesn't leak when it doesn't rain," and "Why do something today if you can put it off till tomorrow?" are mottos of the procrastinator. Procrastinating zaps progress. Only by doing what needs to be done today can you do something else tomorrow. Is there one among us who does not ever procrastinate? Here are a few hints to help us overcome this habit.

1. If you don't want to do a job, divide the job into smaller jobs and do just one of them now.

2. Use the clock to break the job into tolerable amounts.
3. Do something else while you are doing the task you want to put off. I have a sister who will talk on the phone to me while I do jobs I don't want to do.
4. Offer yourself a reward when the task is done.

When we are able to change a self-defeating habit, a wonderful sensation of achievement comes. Acquiring a recharging habit, or finally conquering a destructive one, is a great way of filling up.

7

Unwearyingness

One day, as I was reading in the book of Helaman, a word jumped out at me. I was reading about the time in Book of Mormon history when Nephi, the son of Helaman, preached with vigor to encourage the Nephites to repent. His efforts were mostly unsuccessful, and he was weighed down because of the continuing great wickedness of the people. I can relate to Nephi's feelings. I get weighed down, or fatigued, and feel that my efforts are mostly unsuccessful. (The word *depression* also comes to mind, but since the spectrum of depression is so broad—"I'm depressed; I didn't get in on the sale," to "I'm depressed; I cannot continue to live"—*fatigued* is better.)

Helaman 10:4-5 reads, in part: "Blessed art thou, Nephi, for those things which thou hast done; for I have beheld how thou hast with unwearyingness declared the word, which I have given unto thee, unto this people. . . . And now, because thou hast done this with such unwearyingness, behold, I will bless thee forever."

Unwearyingness. What a word! What does it mean? Roget suggests the following synonyms: *perseverance, endurance, constancy, continuing, steadiness, tenacity, unwavering,* and *relentless.* Certain phrases also come to mind: "Keeps trying," "Puts her shoulder to the wheel," "Hangs in there," "Never gives in," "Never gives out," "Never gives up."

There seems to be an endless variety of bad things which can happen. Tragic events can cause weariness. But even when things go well, we can get weary. If a child makes the honor roll, or a husband gets a promotion, or if we lose five pounds, can we still be weary? The job of living is at times nearly too much for most of us.

The synonyms for *unwearyingness* help us understand how Nephi felt, and the antonyms give us additional insight: *tired, fatigued, worn-out, overused, exhausted, jaded, bushed.* "These adjectives apply to conditions in which physical strength or strength of spirit is depleted, usually as the result of exertion or tribulation. *Tired* is the general, nonspecific term. *Weary,* like *tired,* is applicable to deficiency of strength of spirit, but often carries a stronger implication of discontent resulting from what is burdensome, irksome, or boring." (*The American Heritage Dictionary of the English Language* [New York: American Heritage Publishing Co., 1969], p. 1348.)

Being weary is an unfulfilling feeling. Here are four possible cures for weariness:

1. *Don't expect perfection.* Sometimes we are weary because we expect too much of ourselves. There are no perfect people if "perfect" means "without flaw." But if perfection means being unweary, enduring, trying, there are many who are candidates. We can be perfect for the moment. Whenever we feel imperfect we can ask ourselves, "According to whom am I not perfect?" For example, you can prepare

a perfect breakfast. Perfect may mean that there was food to eat, or that everyone liked what was prepared, or that you prepared a breakfast fit for a king.

2. *Erase the word* should *from your vocabulary.* Sometimes we are weary because there are too many *shoulds.* I should keep a spotless house; I should know exactly how to handle every parenting situation; I should be the ideal wife; I should be totally charitable. I should! I should! If we always respond to the *shoulds* in life, weariness will be our mode. *Could* is a soft, kinder word. *Could* means you are a free agent who makes good choices and decides what to do now and what can wait. *Should* is a hard, demanding taskmaster who rules by the letter of the law. *Could* considers reasons and listens to needs. I am the judge in the *could* versus *should* case daily in my mind.

3. *Take time for yourself.* Sometimes weariness sets in because we think we have to be going and doing for everyone else every minute. One day I was fatigued because I had too much to do. A counselor friend told me it is OK to let the car idle in neutral or park for a few minutes now and then. She said that whenever she feels weary she remembers the car analogy. It spends most of its time traveling forward, but from time to time it goes backward. It spends time at gas stations, repair shops, stop signs, and also in the garage. Like the car, we need to stop for gas—get enough sleep, eat nutritiously, exercise—and go in for routine maintenance—health checkups—and not try to move forward at high speeds all the time.

4. *Experience delight in what you are doing right now.* It's easy to look beyond the moment. "When the baby is toilet trained I'll . . . "; "When the children are married I'll . . . " Tomorrow never comes. Find satisfaction in routines, in faces, in personalities, in you.

These ideas may be cures for weariness, but the scripture in Helaman may suggest another side of the coin.

The Other Side of the Coin

A friend was struggling with the imminent death of two members of her family. One was very old and one was very young. She was a weary counselor in the Young Women program, a tired mother of seven, a fatigued secretary for a one-man business, an exhausted PTA volunteer. She felt the weight of the world. A joint Young Women, Primary, and Relief Society presidency meeting had been called by the bishop. She was depleted but duty convinced her to go. She had come because she *should*, and she expected to be rewarded with gentle, inspiring words to lift her spirits. Soon remarkably ungentle words were burning her ears. "You are capable of more," the bishop was saying. "It's easy to feel put upon. It's convenient to feel you are working to your ability level, but you are really allowing yourself to do less than you can." *Stop! Stop!* she felt like screaming. *Do you realize who you are talking to?* But he continued on, pressing the idea of energetically attacking the world on all fronts, of doing and becoming more.

As my friend told me this story, she said that at first she was angry at the bishop and felt unappreciated. Then she considered the idea that maybe he was right. She asked herself whether she thought that it was her right to feel weary because of her circumstances. She thought of a conversation she had had with some friends—a conversation which turned out to be a one-upmanship complaining session. Could it be fashionable to complain and feel weary? Was feeling weary an excuse? Then she said she began to think that in nearly all aspects of her life there was much, much more to be happy about than to be distressed over. She began to think of ways to make better use of her time, her thoughts, her energy, her talents, her leisure. Even though she felt she had cause to feel down, she decided instead to give herself positive, affirming reminders. She said to herself: "My life is good," "I am happy," "I will enjoy the beauties of the earth." I told her of

52

my experience of reading the word *unwearyingness*, and she agreed that perhaps the difference between Nephi—who received some of the most poetic words and grandest promises from God recorded in the Book of Mormon—and the rest of us is that he resisted being weary. Did Nephi go forward with unwearyingness when others got tired or dissatisfied and gave in to complaining?

Complaining

When I feel like complaining, I can find much to be dissatisfied with. Even when I sacrifice or give service, I can complain about it. I've heard it said that if you complain about the good you do, there is no blessing (see, for example, Moroni 7:6; D&C 70:14). The blessing you might have obtained is spent as you complain. I've murmured about spending whole days in the car, transporting children from seven in the morning to seven in the evening. I've murmured about the cost of mailing packages to our missionary in Spain. I've complained about having to travel nine hundred miles to see my grandchild.

After I read Nephi's words I thought that maybe, like the *un-* which was put in front of *weary*, I should put an *un-* before *complaining*. If I were uncomplaining I would say, "I am blessed to have children. This season of my life will pass, and I will not have anyone to take to lessons and games. It is a privilege to have a driver's license, a car, and resources to do these things." Instead of complaining I could make creative use of time spent in the car.

Should I even think one complaining word about sending packages to Spain, or the money it costs to keep Mike there? My murmuring indicates ingratitude, but I'm honestly, humbly thankful to have a missionary son. I could show an uncomplaining attitude by expressing gratitude for the money to send him packages and the health to allow me to get out of the house and to the post office. And how about my nine-hundred-mile trips? I need to say how wonderful it is to be a grandma—how thankful I am to be able to visit my grandchild. I should be thankful that my grandchild lives in California and not Rangoon. Could I classify any of these inconveniences as sacrifices? Shame on me! Sacrifice is just smart trading—something good for something better—trading up.

It is possible this fashion of complaining got started because of the fear of sounding proud or boastful. How would you react to me if I met you at the post office when I was mailing a package to Spain and I said, "I am so thankful to be the mother of a missionary! I thank the Lord every day. This is one of my greatest blessings." Would you understand that's how I really feel if I instead said, "The contents of this package cost six dollars, and it will probably cost sixteen dollars to mail it to Spain. It sure is expensive to have a missionary." Conversations may be built on the first statement. For example, if I expressed to you my love for my missionary, you might respond by telling me of the love you felt for a missionary in your life, or you might vicariously enjoy my joy. But if I expressed to you my frustration with the cost of mailing the package, you would probably respond by telling me of a similar experience with the high cost of mailing or of some trouble you've had with the postal system. Is it possible to focus on what you are rather than what you aren't, what you've gained rather than what you've lost, and what you have rather than what you are doing without?

Is the idea of sharing a joy the opposite of complaining? My phone rang the other day. "Do you have time for me to tell you something wonderful?" asked my friend Marsha. "Sure!" I said. "Well, I don't have enough people to tell," she hesitatingly apologized. "I can't call heaven." (Her mother and father have passed on.) "I can't call the Philippines." (Her in-laws are on a mission there.) "So I called you." She went on to tell me that her son had won a trip for the whole family to Washington, D.C., by doing a project that took first place in a state competition. Their whole family would get to spend a week in the nation's capital—free. A series of not-so-wonderful things had recently happened to her, and the news of the trip brought great thankfulness and confirmed to her that Heavenly Father was still mindful of them. I felt honored that she chose me to share in her excitement.

Putting an *un-* in front of the words *weary* and *complaining* had fascinating results. What would happen if we took the words *disappointed, grouchy, moody, abrupt, opinionated* and put *un-* in front of each? Would we feel more filled up? Instead of worrying about how fatigued we are and struggling to cope with life, is it possible to build on the positive and cease being weary? Can I find the good in the bad, the light in the darkness, the warmth in the cold, some energy in my apathy, hope in despair, something happy in the sad? Nephi did, and this was his reward:

"Blessed art thou, Nephi, [try filling in your own name] for those things which thou hast done. . . .And now, because thou hast done this with such unwearyingness, behold, I will bless thee forever; and I will make thee mighty in word and in deed, in faith and in works; yea, even that all things shall be done unto thee according to thy word, for thou shalt not ask that which is contrary to my will. Behold, thou art Nephi, and I am God." (Helaman 10:4-6.)

The amazing part of this story is yet to come. Nephi was journeying home and was probably fatigued and hungry at the time he heard the Lord's promise. After the Lord spoke, Nephi had an incredible rebirth of energy. His hunger and fatigue disappeared. Verse twelve states: "And behold, now it came to pass that when the Lord had spoken these words unto Nephi, he did stop and did not go unto his own house, but did return unto the multitudes who were scattered about upon the face of the land, and began to declare unto them the word of the Lord which had been spoken unto him."

8

Competition
That Fills

A few years ago I wrote a book on self-esteem. I felt insecure in my new role as author. I gave one of the first copies to a friend whose approval I needed. When I hadn't heard from her in more than a week, I called to see if she had read it yet. She said she had finished the book and thought it contained some helpful things. "But," she said, "I think there is a problem."

"What's that?" I worried.

"Well," she said, "I think you may become conceited. I've put myself in charge of keeping you humble." I had hoped for a battery charge, but I got drained instead.

A week later another friend called. "I just finished your book," she said enthusiastically, "and I just had to call to tell you it has changed my life." "That's wonderful," I said. "What in the book was so significant?"

"Well . . . " She thought. "It wasn't anything specific. It's just well, it's, well . . . Now you don't intimidate me anymore." Some more of the charge on my battery was gone.

A few weeks after that, the company who published the book had their advertising agent call me. She said they felt that someone sometime may interview me on radio or television. Since I had no experience with such matters, they wanted me to have a practice videotaping session. They had arranged for an anchorwoman to interview me and give me pointers, and they were mailing me a book which would help me prepare.

When the book came, I studied it carefully. I did exactly as it said. I chose my clothes according to the instructions about what to wear on TV. I studied the makeup and hairdo sections. I had my hair cut and wore extra makeup. I had my husband give me practice questions until I felt I could at least make a decent response. At the appointed time I arrived at the advertising agent's office. I was introduced to the anchorwoman, two agents, and a cameraman. The anchorwoman immediately began the interview. After about twenty minutes of questions and answers, she said she'd seen enough.

"Well," she began, "I have to admit that you surprised me. You look so plain, kind of mousy. You answered better than I would expect by just looking at you. But don't worry. I think we can fix you up. Do you have any classy clothes? Any of us here would be glad to go shopping with you to get one outfit which would be suitable. Also, is this the only way you do your hair? My hairdresser, Valentino, would be glad to show you some styles flattering to your face. And Maria, my makeup artist, could help you a lot. Actually," she concluded optimistically, "I think you could be rather pretty." After more of the same, I thanked them and said I was going home to read a good book on self-esteem.

Is There a Shortage?

Sometimes we act as though there is a shortage of battery

power. If your battery is charged, does that mean mine cannot be charged unless I drain some of yours to keep things fair? The experiences I have just related drained me. Were those who drained me more charged up as a result of their actions? I don't think so. It is those we are closest to, our family and friends, who often feel the most competitive with us. Why is it that it is much easier to accept success in strangers?

I looked out of the window one summer morning to see six multicolored hot-air balloons gracefully floating over the Salt Lake Valley. I thought of the elation the balloonists were experiencing. Could no other balloons become airborne because six were already soaring? Of course not. There was sky and morning and a balloon and fuel for thousands more. If someone lifts off or is charged up, it doesn't mean others can't also rise. Some people feel that another's rising will keep them on the ground. Such people seem to feel there is only so much of everything, and if I take some, there is obviously less for them. Just the opposite is true. There is a rising hot-air balloon for everyone. If someone escapes the pull of gravity and soars, all humanity rises a little. But the very nature of life and living keeps everyone's balloon down from time to time. Every season and cycle has deflations. Since soaring for very long is not the nature of life, we should all cheer when anyone succeeds.

Competition

Free enterprise has made America great. Free enterprise competition in business encourages quality products, service and productivity. Competition in the classroom often motivates students to study more and try harder. Competition in sports promotes inner effort. But competition in relationships drains batteries and puts holes in hot-air balloons. If competition becomes a game of keeping up with the Joneses, if peer pressure becomes our motivator, the stage is set for an I'm-not-in-charge-of-anything attack. If we are competing in appearance, or for status, or from fear that if others rise we fall, our relationships will not be as open or as loving or as lasting as otherwise.

I know many people with whom I could feel competition. Joan runs five miles a day; I try to walk one. Nancy's gourmet cooking is a neighborhood legend; I cook things which take no longer to prepare than to consume. Ellan Jean sings like an angel; my talent is enjoying hers. The list could be endless. Everyone I meet could threaten me in one way or another. If I think I don't have value unless I cook, sew, clean, organize, run, sing, look, dress, socialize, and accomplish like the best, I will feel my charge has been zapped. If I am kept busy responding to the pressures to be like someone else, I won't have time to develop my own talents. I can learn from my neighbors and incorporate into my personality any talents I admire in them, if the talents fit me and enhance who I already am. Then my motivation changes from competition to self-improvement, which helps others feel more comfortable around me. Any competitive feelings on their part will decrease. An open, loving, mutually beneficial relationship will be the gift to both of us. Competitive relationships stifle growth, and potential is lost. I can show I feel good about me and about others by just being myself and by replacing one-upmanship, name-dropping, and hints of superiority with sincere compliments. Competition is really an illusion. Reality is who we are and why. If I put on a false face, I am dishonest and I encourage unhealthy competition.

Tale-telling

I can give myself a test to evaluate how competitive I feel. It is simply this: How much time do I spend speaking negatively about other people? I have a friend who continually tells tales about other people, but everything she says is either informative or flattering. I have another friend who also continually tells tales about other people, but everything she says is balanced against herself, her husband, her children, her home, her yard, her calling, and so on. For example, she felt very competitive with her visiting teaching companion. In a futile effort to build herself up she would comment to others on their every difference, always pointing out why she was better than the other woman. I always have the feeling she's talking about me when I'm not present. It's an unfulfilling feeling.

Power

There are ways to generate power in and for yourself. You don't need to compare yourself to anyone. You have the power to do many things:

1. You have the power to be resilient. You can bounce back. You can cope.
2. You have the power to be different, to be yourself and like it, because you are unique—one of a kind.
3. You have the power to be creative. You can be original, artistic, inventive, and imaginative. You can think of and plan ways to do things faster, nicer, more beautifully, with less effort, and more economically.
4. You have the power to be at peace with yourself and to pacify others.
5. You have the power to enjoy—faces, personalities, sunsets, clear nights, new-fallen snow, learning, challenges, differences.
6. You have the power to endure, to last it out, to see it through, to hoe to the end of the row.
7. You have the power to love and let others love you, to give and to receive.

8. You have the power to be productive. You can accomplish, create, do. You can extend yourself and feel good because you are getting at and doing things.
9. You have the power to be appreciative and thankful. You can have a grateful heart.
10. You have the power to be free of competitive feelings.

Being Free

All of the following are consequences of competition: lying, cheating, bearing false witness, boasting, blaming, being critical, gossip, pride, haughtiness, low self-esteem, pettiness, prejudice, jealousy, contention, unhappiness, infidelity, murder, war. The consequences of Laman's and Lemuel's competitive feelings toward Lehi and Nephi comprise the history of the Book of Mormon. For about one thousand years after the competition between Laman and Lemuel and Nephi began, the nations which consisted of the descendants of these men were at war. The same pattern occurred with Jacob and Esau. Will my family split and fragment because of competition I feel with my brothers or sisters? Will my children take sides, see fault, blame, and accuse? Will our neighborhood be divided against itself because of my competitive feelings and actions? The bottom-line trouble with unhealthy competition is that it takes over a person's thoughts, actions, money, time, and emotions and renders the person less able to contribute to society and more likely to use an unfair share of battery power.

The power to be free is realized when we first control, then reduce, then eliminate competitive feelings toward others. When the obstacle of competition is removed from relationships, the following feelings result: warmth, trust, helpfulness, charity, love, humility, camaraderie, healthy self-esteem, unity. Our ideal should be to feel competitive only with our own potential.

Helping Others Rise

When we refuse to be caught in unhealthy competition and honestly present our genuine character to the world, we place ourselves in a position that enables us to lift another.

I am thinking of the family who took in an immigrant German couple at the end of World War II. This family had reason to feel hatred towards Germans, but instead of allowing hatred to control their actions they fed and clothed this couple. They helped them get jobs and arranged for a low-interest loan on a home in their elite neighborhood. Today the German couple has seven children and thirty grandchildren who, as loyal Americans and Latter-day Saints, are contributing and helping others rise.

I am thinking of a sixteen-year-old girl who has a younger brother who is good at everything. He is chosen for this and wins that. His talents are many and varied, and he has a winning personality. Everything he touches turns to figurative gold. But it's his sister who impresses me. She could feel cheated. She could continually try to put holes in his balloon. She could try to hinder him in hopes of building herself up. She could resent him because she struggles at many of the things he's so good at. Instead, she is his biggest fan. She helps him succeed; she congratulates him; she tells others how great he is. I admire her attitude toward him, but there is even more to admire about her. She strives to develop her own talents, and even though in some areas her brother has passed her by, she doesn't let it bother her. She is in competition with herself. She has the same attitude toward her friends, which makes her very popular, but she doesn't seem to notice her popularity.

I am thinking of a young woman who met a young man she wanted to date. They became acquainted. She liked him a lot and tried to get him interested in her. She hoped he would ask her out, but she sensed that her best friend would be much more his equal. She had often felt competitive with her friend. She debated and then overcame her jealous feelings. She introduced the two and they eventually got married.

I am thinking of Laman. What if, when Nephi had challenged him to believe and obey their father, Laman had said, "You are right, Nephi. Even though you are my younger brother, you have great wisdom. Thank you for setting me straight." Think of the historical consequences that would have resulted from that one noncompetitive, unselfish act!

I am thinking of me living next to you. I am wanting to joy in your triumphs, cry in your losses, have patience in our differences, overlook your weaknesses, learn from your strengths, sacrifice when you need me, and talk only of the good about you. I want to let any competitive feelings dissolve as we build each other and a lasting friendship. These are my desires and intentions. Love me, please, even when I fall short. Let's be each other's battery chargers.

9

Celebrations

Celebrations can build self-esteem and unity if memories are made and relationships strengthened. It is good to observe birthdays, anniversaries, promotions, births, deaths, successes, and holidays with appropriate fanfare. Celebrating events can be high points of the year, but celebrating people is more important and more rewarding.

During the two years our son-in-law worked for a company in California, he was responsible for several products with patents pending. One of these products even made the evening news several times. The company received numerous industry awards for our son-in-law's work. Very little was said to him, however, about his successes. He felt great anxiety, because he didn't know his standing; he never was given any reassurance and basically felt underappreciated. He was not celebrated. Meanwhile, his accomplishments did not go unnoticed by other companies. Soon offers were coming in from all over the United States. He decided he could contribute more somewhere else. He gave his bosses notice that he had accepted another job. The bosses were stunned and horrified. For the first week after he told them, they refused to believe it and kept it a secret from all the other employees, fearing the news would cause a mass exodus. They felt so desperate that every morning there was a new offer on his desk. The next to last day he would be there the vice president and chairman of the board of directors invited him to lunch at a local restaurant. Much to our son-in-law's surprise, twenty-four other top employees were invited too. They praised him. They offered him incredible incentives including stock, a promotion, a car, and sixty thousand dollars for a down payment on a house if he would stay. Then the vice president looked at him and said, "Are you really going to go?" When he said he was, the vice president said, "Let's show him how we feel about his decision." All twenty-six got down on their knees, right there in the crowded restaurant, and begged him to stay. What a celebration! But it was too late.

When my daughter told me this story I thought about my celebrations. I discovered I'm best at celebrating events— Christmas, the Fourth of July, Thanksgiving, Easter, Halloween, New Year's, Valentine's, Labor Day, Memorial Day, St. Patrick's and President's days. I know I should celebrate the people more than the event. I should celebrate Christ on Easter and Christmas, the founding fathers on the Fourth of July, the pilgrims on Thanksgiving, our potential on each New Year's Day, those who labor on Labor Day, those who have passed on on Memorial Day. But more important than celebrating national holidays is celebrating the real, living people in our lives by remembering birthdays, anniversaries, retirements, promotions, and so forth. These are days for honoring people near and dear to us. When our daughter Anne was in the fourth grade she brought home a paper on which she had written all of her favorite things. Under "favorite holiday" she had written "December fourth—my birthday." How would she have felt if December fourth was a day I let slip by?

People

People should be celebrated at milestones in their lives—birth, baptism and confirmation, birthdays, graduations, marriage, childbirth, anniversaries, retirement, and death. These are personal events that traditionally deserve to be noted and truly observed. But the kind of celebrating I want to do more of isn't marked on a calendar. I want to celebrate the routine. When I think of the people I admire, love, and appreciate in my family, neighborhood, and ward—people who I don't celebrate often enough or well enough—I feel sad. When I neglect to celebrate, I wonder if my husband and children know how I feel about them. How can I better celebrate them? How often should I celebrate them—once a year on a birthday, once a day? I wonder if in unhappy homes divorce and waywardness are ways of saying, "I haven't been celebrated. I feel underappreciated. I want to go live with (or work for) someone else." I think of the people I serve with in the Church. They deserve more than a quick thanks now and then. How do I celebrate them?

I know that some of the problems in our home have come as a result of not enough people-celebrating. Several times during my life as a mother I have felt communication barriers like prison walls between a child and me. During an especially difficult time, I prayed for a way to improve the situation. A simple idea came. Each time I saw that child I would smile at him. A smile is a very simple celebration which tells another person that I notice him and at least like him well enough to give him a smile. This gesture repeated over and over helped to melt the barrier between my child and me. I asked some of my friends how they celebrate the people in their homes on days other than holidays. They mentioned writing notes of praise and thanks, giving compliments, saying thanks, remembering likes and dislikes, offering help, putting surprises under pillows or in lunch sacks, taking time—all the time it takes—to listen, being there at times of need and at comings and goings, and celebrating accomplishments. The women I asked agreed that it is very difficult to celebrate another well enough and often enough.

One idea a mother suggested was to use each child's name with respect. She suggested that a child's name should be used with dignity, like the names of royalty, and only for positive purposes. I've often used a child's full name when he or she was annoying me or was in trouble. This mother hinted that taking anyone's name in vain was wrong.

One day I complimented our exchange student, Margarita. She responded, "Oh, you see me with good eyes." I like the idea. I need to see my husband, children, friends, and my surroundings with good eyes, because celebrating each other is a refueling experience. A few weeks before our daughter Liz was to begin life at BYU, four of her roommates called from California. They had made the effort of a conference call to introduce themselves. When I told them Liz was out of town, they were disappointed. So I said, "Tell me about yourselves." They decided amongst themselves who should go first. Jen began telling facts about herself. Then the others contributed things that she wouldn't say about herself. "She's very thoughtful." "She'll be the one to keep the apartment clean." "She's cute." Then it was Amy's turn, and the same thing happened. Each one had many nice things to say about the others. Mutual admiration societies celebrate each member; they see each other with good eyes.

We can also celebrate groups—our family, our ward, our company, our state, our nation. We can take a lesson from schools which generate great pride and loyalty by using slogans. Our high school's mascot is the eagle. Often the marquee in front of the school says something about "eagle pride." A friend shared with me a way she and her husband have built pride and unity in a traditional celebration of their family. After every family home evening, they join hands and coil up together like a snail and shout, "Family hug!" A family home evening lesson suggests celebrating by chanting, "The ___ family is the best family ever."

Worship

When I looked in the thesaurus for words that describe *celebrate*, I was surprised that *worship* was a synonym. That suggested to me another group of people I feel a need to celebrate—the Godhead. But how does a mortal celebrate omniscient, perfect, eternal people? I looked back at the list of ideas for celebrating mortals and found that those ideas work for immortals too. I can write notes of praise, which in scripture are called psalms. I can give members of the Godhead compliments in my prayers. I can show thanks in word and action. I can remember their likes and dislikes—they like people who keep their commandments, who express gratitude, and who don't sin. I can take time to listen for promptings after prayer and to listen for the still, small voice. I can be willing to serve when they need me. I can reverence their names. I celebrate them as I learn about their accomplishments by reading the scriptures, attending the temple, and appreciating their creations. I celebrate them as I contemplate my opportunities past, present, future, and in eternity. My greatest celebration of them comes as I serve (celebrate) my brothers and sisters. It is a fulfilling feeling to celebrate the Creator, his Father, and the Holy Ghost. Michael McLean must have been thinking these thoughts as he wrote the words, "Celebrating the light, the light of the world."

The gospel is full of phrases that suggest celebrating life. Undoubtedly we were among those who shouted for joy at the Savior's birth. A multitude of us was given the opportunity to sing, "Glory to God in the highest." We sing in our homes and meetings: "Rejoice, the Lord is King!" (*Hymns*, 1985, no. 66.) "Come, rejoice, the King of glory / Speaks to earth again. . . . / Shout hosanna to his name; / One and all his might proclaim." (*Hymns*, no. 9.) "Now let us rejoice. . . . / Good tidings are sounding." (*Hymns*, no. 3.) "What glorious scenes mine eyes behold! / What wonders burst upon my view!" (*Hymns*, no. 16.) "On this day of joy and gladness, / Lord, we praise thy holy name" (*Hymns*, no. 64). "There is sunshine . . . there is music . . . there is springtime . . . there is gladness in my soul today." (*Hymns*, no. 227.)

The scriptures contain hundreds of references to the joyful events past, present, and future worthy of celebrating. King David is one of our best examples of one who celebrated God and all his creations. From Psalm 28:7, "The Lord is my strength and my shield; my heart trusted in him, and I am helped: therefore my heart greatly rejoiceth; and with my song will I praise him."

In reflective moments of worship I feel there is a psalm within me waiting to be written. But the way life rises and falls in peaks and valleys, before I take the time to write a celebration of my Heavenly Father something happens to take my attention away. I admire King David because he did take the time to record his rejoicings. Here is an outline that can be used to write a psalm of praise in scripture form. I've used words and phrases liberally from David's psalms.

Psalm of _____ (your name)

1. Please give ear to my words, O Lord. Consider my thoughts.
2. Thou art my King and my God, and unto thee I pray this song of praise.

3. Listen to the voice of my thankful heart.
4. Thou wast there when I needed thee when
   _____ and _____.
5. Thou hast blessed me with many roles—that of
   _____, _____, _____, and
   _____. I thank thee for these opportunities.
6. I praise thy name for clothing my spirit in my physical body. I marvel at _____, _____, and
   _____.
7. Thy counsels and laws for a fruitful life are written in thy sacred writ. How wondrous and great are the words of thy prophets! I ponder the words of _____, and I am filled.
8. I go into thy holy house, thy temple, and say in my heart _____.
9. What am I that thou art mindful of me and that I am worthy of all these blessings? I am so much lower than the angels, yet thou dost hear my voice.
10. Lead me, O Lord, in thy righteousness because of my weaknesses. Help me to _____.
11. The Lord hath heard my supplication; the Lord will receive my prayer. Thanks be to God whose goodness surpasseth all.

Me

I wondered what else I could celebrate in order to fill up and recharge. How about celebrating me! Isn't that a way of worshipping Heavenly Father? I am the creation of his with which I am most familiar. I could make a list of things I can rejoice in about myself. What do I like about me physically, intellectually, emotionally, spiritually, as a woman, wife, mother, worker in the Church, friend, and relative?

I can celebrate me by rejoicing in the many things I can do. I can go to school, the library, a lecture, a travelogue, a play, the ballet, the opera. I can read a book, the newspaper, a magazine. I can use a camera, a vacuum, a computer, a curling iron. I can give a hug, smile at a child, take a casserole to a neighbor. I can look up scriptures, relate them to my life, and even memorize a few. I can learn to swim or play golf or tennis, or I can try snow-skiing and water-skiing. I can appreciate art and study the life of a famous artist. I can learn to lead music. I can sing in a choir. I can have a song in my heart all day. I can make other people feel good about themselves. I can listen. I can start a resource file containing ideas, famous quotes, poems, thoughts, and stories. I can organize, tidy, clean, beautify. I can go the extra mile. I can do many things. I will celebrate me!

10

The Sandwich Syndrome

One morning I was driving down a scenic, narrow country road in England. Suddenly in front of me was a long line of cars. In the next thirty minutes I inched up close enough to see that the cab of an eighteen-wheeled truck was stuck under a train bridge. The old bridge had suffered quite a bit of damage, and loose bricks lay scattered on the road. Several large cracks in the bridge made it look as if it would collapse if the truck were moved.

As I got closer I saw that when the other cars reached the truck they would wait until no traffic was coming and then pass the truck. I watched twenty or so cars take their turn to wait and watch and go around the truck. It was scary because the train bridge was deep and, with the curve in the road, visibility was very limited. In my rearview mirror I saw cars lined up behind me for miles. My turn finally came. I pulled slightly out to the side of the truck as the others had done. I waited for an oncoming car. I was ready to pass the truck when suddenly it began to back up. I honked my car's horn, thinking that surely the truck would stop. I honked the horn again. I had three preschoolers with me, and they all began to scream. The car behind me began to honk. There was no place to go—an eighteen-wheeled monster was backing into us and a mile-long chain of cars was stacked behind. We were the filling in a sandwich just waiting to be chewed; we were in a vice and about to be crushed. I was ready to throw the children out of the car and jump out myself, but then the truck stopped. The car looked like an accordion, but we were safe. I felt I had just been rescued from a torture chamber with walls that move toward each other.

Since that time I have watched to see if sandwiching is something that happens not only with peanut butter and jelly and in strange auto accidents but also in daily life. Being sandwiched is a totally out-of-control feeling. I hate the feeling of being sandwiched! Most of life's unpleasant surprises— sickness, death, divorce, crime, sin—create sandwiching situations. We can be sandwiched between the past and present, between two choices at the fork in a road, between needs or wants and limited resources. We can be torn between the devil and God or between a poor choice and its consequences. We can be caught between a poor product and a company, between a financial stress and a moral right, between time and responsibility, between fatigue and duty, between work and home, between life and death. Even well-meaning people can cause us to feel sandwiched. We can be sandwiched between a spouse and a mother-in-law, a spouse and a child, a boss and a fellow employee, two children, or two friends. A mother is often sandwiched between her work load and personal needs, and between children's and husband's needs.

One day I started to make a list of my problems and the things I'd like to change. They were all situations in which I was the filling in some sandwich. I noticed that the tighter the squeeze the less in charge and filled up I felt. In trying to analyze how to rid myself of sandwiching situations I discovered that all sandwiching situations are not bad.

Between a Rock and a Hard Place

Some sandwiching situations are good and necessary. There are choices we make in which we purposely place ourselves between a rock and a hard place. Such choices occur when we take risks. Every risk is a potential sandwich. Being too afraid or too reticent to take risks may limit our opportunities for growth. We cannot see around any corner, so if we never stick our necks out we will miss out. There will be choices we make that carry risks clearly worth taking because the potential for success outweighs the possibility for failure. Sometimes, however, we will take great risks because our needs or another's dependence on us challenge us to meet that need. Pursuing a degree despite limited time, money, and/or ability and starting a business with little capital and substantial debt are two examples of sandwiches which may produce progress and growth. The greatest risks offer the greatest possibility of gain or success, but they also offer the greatest possibility of loss or failure.

The difference between wise risk taking and stressful sandwiching is choice. The more I can choose, the more in charge and filled up I feel. This has been true since our premortal life. Satan's plan took away our free agency and sandwiched us. God's plan offered us the freedom to choose for ourselves. When we allow others to choose their own sandwiches, they feel more in control. When choosing a risk, a potential sandwich, the better we anticipate possible consequences—loss of time, money, respect, and future options—

the less sandwiching we'll have to endure. Even so, there will be situations in which our best thought-out plans have a surprise or two lurking in them—like my trip through the English countryside.

Appraising the Risks

A good way to decide whether the sandwiching consequences of an action justify taking it is to calculate the cost. One of my good friends is a teacher. She teaches next door to one of her very good friends. One day the fire drill bell rang while both teachers were in their rooms correcting papers. They were tired and decided that since they'd gone outside for fire drills for fifteen years, it wouldn't hurt to stay in this time. They both went back to correcting tests. Five or so minutes had passed when the sound of doors opening and closing startled both teachers. They had forgotten that the principal and fire marshall would go through every classroom to see if it had been vacated according to code. Panic struck the teachers. How foolish they would look and how hard it would be to explain why they had not left their rooms. My friend ran to her back door. The other teacher was already there. What should they do? They decided to hide. They could hear the voices of the two men getting closer. The moment was tense. The men entered my friend's room. They saw the windows closed, the lights off, and the door to the adjoining room open—the room where the two rapidly greying teachers were hiding. They were not discovered, but there is a valid lesson to be learned from this incident. Early in the decision-making process we need to appraise the risks by asking ourselves, "What might this cost?" If the consequences seem inconsequential, perhaps you will choose to risk more. If the cost is potentially high, you may look for alternatives so as to avoid being sandwiched between a poor choice and its consequences.

Feeling Unnecessarily Sandwiched

Unrealistic expectations create sandwiches in life. If I expect my children to be perfect, if I expect my marriage to be completely harmonious, if I expect to stay youthful forever, if I equate problems in life with something I have done wrong, then I put myself between two slices of bread—expectations and reality. If I expect my husband to help with the children, be a good cook, be an expert gardener, never lose his hair, never gain a pound, never age, never raise his voice, always be sensitive to my feelings, bring me gifts, and earn enough money for all my wants, this dream becomes one side of the bread and reality the other. When it dawns on me that my unrealistic expectations are the reason for the sandwich I'm uncomfortably in, I think, "This is stressful. How can I get out of this sandwiching situation?" Then I remember the solution—just refuse to be the filling and join up with one slice of bread or the other. How can I refuse to be the filling between expectations and reality? There are probably many ways, but celebrating life for what it is rather than clinging to the dream of what it isn't works best for me. For example, if I have unrealistic expectations of marriage, I can realign. And in some ways reality, though different from expectations, has proven to be better!

One Sure Way Out

Sandwiches create adversarial situations. If someone has to be right, that makes the other person wrong. If there's a winner, there must also be a loser. In some sandwiching situations there is a way out that saves us negotiation, compromise, suffering in silence, or any of the host of other responses to the feeling of being trapped. The way out consists of realizing that if we can't change the situation, we can change ourselves.

Count the Cost

Nathaniel Hawthorne's story "The Birthmark" is a tale of a chemist who thinks his wife is nature's perfection. She is stunningly beautiful except for a small birthmark on her cheek. As the years pass he becomes obsessed with the birthmark. He must have perfection; the birthmark must go. He tells his wife he has discovered a way to make the birthmark disappear. She asks him what he will do if he finds that it is connected to her heart. He finally convinces her to let him try. He administers a drug to her. As the days pass she becomes weak, and the birthmark remains. He increases the dosage. In the end the birthmark is gone but so is her life, for he has poisoned her. He did not appraise the risk nor count the cost. Fear and obsessions may be the underlying cause of unnecessary risk taking.

Actuaries are trained to count the cost for insurance companies. Through statistical information, they calculate what the chance of every possible mishap is. They know what the risk is for babies to die at birth, for smokers and nonsmokers to get lung cancer, for bikers to get hit by cars, for lightning to strike. As a woman I need to know what risks I may encounter, so that I can make wise choices. A friend of mine takes vitamins by the dozens daily but will not wear her seat belt. Another acquaintance won't let her children jump on trampolines but lets them roller blade without wearing any protective gear. We have an obligation to ask the questions and learn the facts—to know what the risks really are.

Too often women are sandwiched because of a lack of money, information, time, and assertiveness. How to earn money and how to make it work for you are two important skills women need. I was raised to anticipate that a man would take care of me financially. Statistics tell us that only three percent of women live in a traditional home—a home with children, a father, and a mother who does not work outside the home. Most of the homeless population consists of women with children. Our girls need to know how to earn money. The ideal situation is for each of them to be able to stay at home with their children if they possibly can and if they choose to but also to be prepared to step into the job market if they do need to. Tied into the issue of earning a living is the problem of women who have not the foggiest idea of how to be assertive enough to make the phone calls, gather the information, and see the people they need to in order to make the systems work for them. Time is another barrier for women with children. Who cares for the children if she has to work? Who pays for the baby-sitter or day care? Who repairs the car? Who unclogs the drain? Who waters the lawn? Girls need the same training as boys to prepare them for their adult futures.

I have been a working mother and know that working mothers are sandwiched on many sides. A single working mother has infinitely more pressures. The more sandwiched a woman is the fewer the options that tend to be open to her. How can we help our teenage girls avoid becoming members of the poorest and most sandwiched segment of society? In my opinion we need to teach young women to be assertive and to get a good education. They need to be prepared for careers, yet hopefully they will choose, if possible, to stay at home.

It is a risk to work outside the home if you don't need to. The risk comes because a prophet has given direction concerning the subject. I heard the testimony of a forty-year-old woman who felt sandwiched between her choice of working outside the home and President Benson's counsel. Janice (I'll call her) has five children, ages seven to seventeen. Her husband makes an adequate living. Janice went to work seven years ago to keep her children in fashionable clothes and music lessons. When President Benson gave his talk counseling women to stay at home with their children wherever possible, Janice searched her soul, prayed, and fasted. With much anxiety, she quit her job. The next six months were torture as she saw no benefits in her new lifestyle. She was bored, and adjusting to one income seemed impossible. One day she got a call from her seventeen-year-old daughter's seminary teacher. He told her that in a testimony meeting that morning her daughter had said these words: "We have had the greatest past six months in our family." Then as tears began trickling down her face the daughter had said, "My mother came home."

11

Giving and Receiving Criticism

One day I was sitting on the piano bench with one of our children. I was helping her practice. Suddenly she burst into tears, sobbing that all I did was tell her what she was doing wrong. "Nobody's perfect," she chided. So, we had a little chat about the role of criticism in her life. I asked her if she would rather have me or her teacher tell her she was forgetting all the B-flats in a piece. I asked her what the consequence of going to her lesson and not playing the B-flats was. She said she'd have to take the piece another week. Then we talked about how in her ballet class her teacher corrected her positions at the barre. A week before, her teacher had placed her in front of the mirror so my daughter could see how her wrists and elbows felt and looked when rounded in high fifth. After she had seen the difference in the mirror she could assume the right position by herself. Finally she realized that when she used the criticisms she received, she improved.

What does criticism have to do with being filled up? How should we react to criticism and the critic? How can we give criticism so that it is helpful and effective? Is it possible for us to respond to others' words, faces, reactions, and subtle suggestions so that direct criticism is rarely necessary?

I asked ten people how they felt about being criticized. Six of the ten said they hated to be criticized. They suggested that the world would be a better place without any criticism. Several referred to the mote and beam story in the New Testament. Others quoted Jesus: "Judge not, that ye be not judged" (Matthew 7:1). They talked about criticism as being damaging to self-esteem and ego. They said they felt persecuted when they were criticized. To these six people, criticism was all negative. But when I asked if they ever gave criticism, they changed the word *criticism* to something like *helpful suggestions*.

The other four people I talked to had an opposite view of criticism. One told the following story. He and his wife had been out with friends. As they were getting ready for bed his wife said, "You acted like a fool tonight." Pow! He felt he had been shot. He thought of finding fault with something she had done. Then he thought of acting hurt and pouting. Finally he thought, "She may be right." Even though he didn't like the message, his confidence in her (the messenger) and his desire not to offend her made him open to the potential for change and growth. Another person suggested that criticism is inherently neither good nor bad. She said you should view all criticism as opinion and consider it an opportunity to see the world from someone else's perspective.

When we receive criticism the message may hurt and the time, word, and place choices of the messenger may be completely inappropriate. But no matter how the message is sent or by whom, criticism can be a commodity of high value. It does let you see the world from another's perspective. It may be the catalyst to help you break out of the doldrums and take advantage of an ignored talent or to help you realize something about yourself that offends others. Criticism is like a gift. It may be handed to you wrapped in newspaper. It may be left unwrapped on your doorstep. It may be wrapped in satin and given with fanfare. You may choose whether or not to open the gift. You may not find the gift useful. You may throw it away. You may despise the giver. You may return the gift. You may keep the gift to give to someone else. You may cherish the gift and thank the giver. To be filled up we need to know how to give and receive criticism.

Receiving Criticism

There are many destructive ways we can respond to criticism:

1. We can feel hurt and counter with our own criticisms.
2. We can retaliate with a machine gun of verbiage or pout and use the silent treatment.
3. We can block out the criticism, refusing to admit that it is valid, and hear nothing.
4. We can make an excuse and say, "Yes, but . . . "
5. We can fake agreement but actually brew resentment.
6. We can withdraw and feel persecuted.
7. We can magnify the criticism a hundredfold, blowing it completely out of proportion as in O. Henry's story "A Piece of String." In the story a man picks up a piece of string on the road. He is later accused of picking up and keeping a wallet. Even though he is cleared of all charges, he spends his life retelling the injustice. He dies with the words, "It was just a piece of string," on his lips.

In each of the seven destructive styles listed above, the person responds in such a way that he or she does not have to deal with the criticism. It's a convenient side step, a distraction, a detour to keep from facing the fact that perhaps a change would be for the better. A hostile reaction to all criticism prevents personal progress. If we are willing to receive criticism, we show an attitude of acceptance. We feel good enough about ourselves to listen to another's thoughts about us.

There is certainly much destructive criticism dished out. It may be sarcastic, random, meaningless, spiteful, or unjust. It may come just because we are in the wrong place at the wrong moment. It may come because we are the next step down in someone's pecking order. It may come when we are expecting praise or when we are tired or sick. We may not like the message or the messenger's bedside manner. Of course, we shouldn't change something about ourselves just because someone criticizes us. There are people who are expert faultfinders. Their negative view of the world classifies them as suspicious, grudge-filled, pessimistic persons who act as if they want to make others as miserable as they are. If you live or work with one of these persons, hopefully you can find ways to help him or her see the world as a friendlier place. These people who make incorrect, unkind statements for the wrong reasons need the example of someone who gives and receives criticism positively. We should not reinforce the destructive-criticism habit by responding negatively.

Just as we shouldn't automatically change for any criticism given, neither should we throw up barriers that prevent us from hearing, seeing, understanding, and learning from what is said. So whether the criticism comes in a positive or negative way, whether or not you feel it is given destructively or constructively, you can control your response to it even though you may feel rejection and want to strike back—

shoot the messenger and disregard the message. The only good defense is to control both emotion and reaction, and there are various ways to achieve such control. If the criticism is random, such as that from a stranger yelling a name from a passing car or a salesclerk being brusque, let it roll off. Don't allow it to penetrate. It means nothing. Brush it off. Forgive and forget. If the criticism comes from someone you deal with often:

1. Listen carefully and realize the critic is letting you see into a window of himself.
2. Analyze your critic. Does he know the facts? What are his motives? Does he have the skills and qualifications to make a good judgment? Is his judgment a whim? Are you merely the next victim in a pecking order?
3. If you decide the criticism is invalid, respond politely and let it go. You need not explain or excuse yourself.
4. If you decide the criticism has merit, act on it appropriately. You may even want to thank your critic.
5. Know that being criticized doesn't mean you are bad, stupid, or unlovable or that you have failed. The criticism may open up your mind to alternative, creative ways to change and improve. Sometimes you may want to make a change, not because it is necessarily a better way but because it helps someone.

Criticisms I Want to Receive

Sometimes it takes courage to give criticism. There are simply some areas that require the messenger to be skillful and tactful if he is to deliver the message kindly. But sometimes the message is so important that it's better said coarsely than not at all. For example: I want to know if I have body or mouth odor problems; I want to know if I turn people off by interrupting them; I want to know if my laugh is insincere or my voice high and irritating; I want to know if I am not magnifying a talent. If I'm bossy, argumentative and opinionated, or indecisive and wimpy, help me see that there are more effective ways of relating to people. You can help me by being my mirror, but please tell me my faults just once.

Criticisms I Don't Want to Receive

Conversely, I don't want to know that you don't like the dress I am wearing (unless you are my husband or child and you tell me before I go out for the evening). I don't want to know that you don't like someone in my family. I don't want to know the negative things you remember about my past. I don't want to be told that my chin is pointed, that my ears are too big, or that my shoulders are too wide. Please tell me about things I have control over—things I can change.

Giving Criticism

When giving criticism make a plan:

1. Know what behavior you want the person to change.

2. Decide if the behavior is troublesome enough that it is worth taking the risk of offending the person.

3. Try shaping first. Shaping is an alternative to criticism. "Dan, you greeted Mrs. Norton at the door better than a butler would have. You called her by name and invited her to sit down. You were very polite." This comment to our ten-year-old shows how I want to shape his behavior. I want him to be polite. So whenever he gets close to being polite I use his name and give sincere praise. ("Dan, you greeted Mrs. Norton at the door better than a butler would have.") I follow with words that describe how a polite person answers the door. ("You called her by name and invited her to sit down.") Step three is to state a specific word that identifies the quality

you are shaping. ("You were very polite.") Hopefully, Dan then thinks in his mind, "Oh, I am a polite person. Being polite is good."

4. If at this point you still feel the person can be helped by the criticism you want to make, ask yourself whether it is realistic and possible for the change to be made.

5. Decide how, when, and where you can give this criticism so that it will have the greatest chance of being accepted. Avoid the four nevers:
   —Never criticize in the heat of the moment.
   —Never add on to another criticism. "Well, since we are on the subject . . . "
   —Never criticize in haste.
   —Never criticize in anger.

6. Emphasize the positive. Sandwich the criticism between thick slices of sincere, accurate praise.

7. Be specific. A generalized statement won't help. "You are not polite." What does *polite* mean to you? What does it mean to him/her?

8. Be empathetic. Ask yourself, "How would I like this message delivered to me? Would I want to be criticized at this moment in this situation?"

9. Don't attack with "you" messages. Send "I" messages. "I feel . . . "

10. Make it simple. Don't repeat yourself or belabor the point. This is how the lecture got its bad reputation.

11. Show how changing the behavior will bring benefit to him/her. Use the magic art of emotional appeal, and show the person how he will benefit from the change. "You prepare your oral reports so carefully, and your voice is so pleasing to your listeners! A little more eye contact would make it even more effective."

12. Prepare the person for a positive response to your criticism. "I know I can say this to you, because I know you will take it well."

13. Simply stated, helpful criticism is given in the right way at the right time at the right place by someone who cares. It is specific and whenever possible includes not only what is wrong but also possible ways to correct it.

14. Try using rewards or incentives to encourage change.

15. Phrase creatively. Use language that indicates that with a slight change imperfections will become perfections. "Your presentation was so close to being perfect. Could you just . . . "

16. Be brave and ask for feedback after the criticism is delivered. Determine whether the message you sent arrived.

17. Remember that the only purpose of criticism is to have the message accepted to the extent that it will be acted upon and a change made.

18. Planning and timing are crucial.

19. Ask yourself, "Am I expecting too much?" and "Am I being too negative?" Destructive criticism is useless. Such criticism yields no change and may damage your relationship with the person.

Developing these skills is a lifelong effort. As I gracefully give and receive criticism I increase my feelings of being filled up and charged up.

12

Compressing and Extending Life

At the end of a particularly wearing day, I thought momentarily of how glad I was that the day was over. Then I stopped myself and realized that one more of the days of my life had been spent. I felt hypocritical. I want to be *filled* up not *used* up. A quote from everyone's favorite cat, Garfield, says, "If life's a bridge to be crossed, let's dawdle all we can." I understand the intent of the statement—eat lasagna, chase Odie, and sleep. Such a life may sound appealing, but since everyone's days are numbered, perhaps we should seek ways to compress minutes to give more productive hours and to compact hours to yield more fruitful days. If the boring, repetitious, mundane, and routine elements of life can be scrunched and if ways to enhance life can be found, then there will be more time for life's essence—the relationships, the creativity, the adventures. We will be filled up with higher quality and quantity of life. There are probably hundreds of creative and wise ways to find more life to live and to live it to its fullest extent. Here are a few to get you thinking of possibilities.

Eliminating the Repetitious, Mundane, and Unnecessary

1. I spend lots of time searching for lost items. If I could eliminate losing things, I'd gain time on the bridge. I'm sure I will continue to misplace items and forget the "safe" places I put things, but if I can discipline myself to put things where they belong, I'll save time and extend life. A secret for me is being willing to discard things. Then, at least, I have less to look through. The worst part about hunting for something is the stress I feel because of the time and opportunity being lost. As I try to eliminate the need to look for lost things, I punish myself if I do lose something by forcing myself to clean out whatever I have to look through in the process of finding the item.

2. I want to eliminate from life as much sickness and accident as possible for myself and my family. Prevention allows me to avoid unnecessary events. Illness and accident are big subtraction signs in the sum of life. A friend who recently spent fifteen thousand dollars and one week in the hospital because of a heart attack wishes he had spent that ounce of prevention rather than the pound of cure. At his discharge the doctor said, "Walk every day and lose twenty-five pounds and you'll be just fine." If my friend had been doing that all along, he'd be seven days and fifteen thousand dollars richer. Annual physical exams, preventative tests, good nutrition, cardiovascular exercise, defensive driving, avoiding unnecessary risk, reading directions, and taking precautions will save time that may otherwise be lost to accident and disease.

3. I am working on eliminating my fear of change. Buddha said, "Each man must build his life on an awareness that nothing lasts, that everything is subject to change." Life is a series of cycles. Change is the one constant, the one thing that always will occur. Feeling stressed and fearing change are usually harder on us than adjusting and coping. Change is going to happen whether we like or want it or not. We belong to a church which believes in change—change in the form of revelation, opportunity, growth. A testimony of the inevitability, universality, and fortuity of change helps us feel fulfilled.

4. I want to eliminate worry over things that never happen. Such thoughts are easy to identify because they usually begin with the words *what if*. Fear prevents me from being a productive person. It zaps battery power. It makes me feel unfulfilled. Worry is both unproductive and destructive— unproductive because the things I worry about seldom happen and destructive because it causes stress and lost thought time. I've heard that a good way to eliminate fear is to laugh it out of existence. Fear can't coexist with laughter. Keeping busy is another technique that helps me worry less. Worry shows an absence of faith. Fear robs opportunity. The story of the youngest child in a large family—a child who worries that he'll never get enough—illustrates worry's rewards. One day the mother offers everyone a cookie from the jar. He is the last to reach his hand in. There's just one cookie left, and it is slightly broken. His fear becomes reality as in despair he throws the cookie on the floor and cries, "My cookie's all broke."

5. I waste time by making thoughtless remarks I later have to apologize or make reparations for. If I swallow that harsh, unkind, or sarcastic word, I can then spend time building rather than repairing relationships. There is a trap I call the Soap Opera Syndrome; it makes people think something always has to be wrong in their relationships. One situation just about gets worked out when another problem complicates life. We can't afford to waste our time on the bridge in this tail-chasing cycle. Repenting takes time, but feeling

guilty takes even more time. Repenting saves time that would be spent in feeling guilty. Avoiding the negative act in the first place saves both the feeling-guilty and the repenting time.

6. I allow self-defeating thoughts to take time. Here in Utah we have a campaign to make Utah a litter-free state. The slogan is "Don't waste Utah." Likewise I should say, "Don't waste me." I waste me by taking myself too seriously and thinking negative thoughts. These actions defeat me by subtracting time on the bridge. If I find the litter of negative or defeating thoughts cluttering my mind, I need to discipline myself and replace those thoughts with ones that are upbeat, new, fun, and happy.

Random Ideas for Enhancing Time on the Bridge

1. *Enjoy right now!* Spencer Johnson has written many books that discuss things you can do in one minute. It's a fun exercise once in a while to see just what you can do in one minute. Johnson also wrote a book, *The Precious Present*, which can be read in fifteen minutes. The word *present* is used as a pun to mean both "right now" and "a gift." The gift is now. It isn't the past or the future. It's not in waiting or remembering. It's what can be appreciated, felt, loved, seen, believed, heard, tried, sensed, observed, given, shared, or experienced in this moment. Nothing matters more than what is done with each present of sixty seconds. Thomas Carlyle said, "Our main business is not to see what lies dimly at a distance, but to do what lies clearly at hand."

2. *Look at burdens as blessings.* Perhaps you've read the story of a group of men attempting to climb Mount Everest. One slips and is seriously injured. A close friend volunteers to carry him down. A guide leads the way. The descent is treacherous, especially to the man with the burden on his back. The ice seems like glass, and the wind whips snow at

such a velocity that at every step he is almost thrown off balance. The guide, on the other hand, seems to have an easy time and often has to wait. Even though the temperature is many degrees below freezing, the man with the burden gets hot and sweaty. He wants to rest; he hopes the guide will offer to carry the burden for a while. Suddenly, just a few feet from the base camp, the guide falls down. The other man sets down his burden to check on the guide. The guide is dead—frozen stiff. He had no burden to keep him warm and alive.

Carrying burdens can be a blessing to us, and sharing the burdens can extend the blessings to others. If the burden in the story had been shared, the guide would have lived. One day a teacher brought into a classroom a stack of one-foot-square chalkboards. It was an extremely heavy burden. She asked everyone to take one chalkboard and pass the stack on. As the burden was passed around the room and each person took a chalkboard from the stack, the burden became lighter and lighter. We can bless ourselves and each other by carrying and sharing burdens.

3. *Water your neighbor's lawn.* One side of our lawn never stays green. Our neighbor's lawn, which adjoins ours, is always green. In the past I have been very careful to water only our side, because theirs doesn't need it. This year I realized that watering just our side didn't work. I changed the sprinklers so they watered well over onto our neighbor's side. Of course, it worked and now you can't tell where their side ends and ours begins. Our lawn has never looked so good.

I heard the story of three sisters who entered a contest to win a thousand-dollar wardrobe. One of the sisters actually won. She decided it would only be fair to divide her prize with her sisters and give $333.33 to each. When she told her sisters of her decision, they felt great love for her and thanked her for her generosity, but insisted that she keep all the money for herself. This woman wanted to water her sisters' lawns, and her own got watered as well.

4. *Anticipate that good things will be sent your way.* Two groups of people lived on opposite sides of an island. Neither group was aware of the other's presence. The people on one side of the island had a problem: there was no way to dispose of garbage. Finally the town council decided to load barges with the garbage and send them out into the open sea. The ocean currents were such that the barges loaded with garbage soon made their way around the island. One morning the people on the opposite side found the smelly barges on their beautiful white beach. These people were confused by the mysterious "gift," but they knew what to do. They got rid of the garbage and in its place put fresh fruits, vegetables, and beautiful flowers. On the leading barge they put a sign that read, "We, too, send our very best," and they pushed the barges out to sea.

5. *Respond to the unusual.* Richard and I were invited to a wedding breakfast last summer. I picked him up at work and drove the two blocks to the hotel where the breakfast was being held. We tried to park in the hotel parking terrace, but it was full. We drove next door to the parking terrace of a large mall. It was a very busy noon hour, and we had to go to the seventh level to find a parking place. From the time that we had been about a block away from the hotel we had been aware of an alarm ringing. When we got out of the car, the sound of the alarm was even louder. At first we thought it was a car alarm, but it was too loud to be that. And it wasn't a burglar alarm, because the alarm would sound and stop in what seemed like a signal or code. We walked to the elevator and saw the alarm that was ringing. The sign on it read, "If this alarm rings, notify police immediately." I assumed, with the hundred, even thousands, of people who were in the area, that for sure someone had called the police and that the alarm was just stuck.

From the experience of living with my husband for twenty-six years I should have anticipated that he would find out what was happening. He has enriched our lives many times by responding to the unusual. We walked down the stairs, and Richard told me to wait. He walked down to the parking attendant in the hotel parking terrace and asked him to call 911. The attendant replied, "This matter doesn't concern me. The alarm is in the mall parking terrace." Richard came back and we walked into the hotel. He went to a phone to call the police himself. The phone wasn't working. Then he went to the desk clerk and told her about the situation. She asked, "What do you want me to do about it?" He said, "Don't you have an emergency number for the mall?" She searched. Finally she found a number and called. Richard waited while she told the security guard that a customer was reporting that someone was stuck in the mall parking terrace elevator.

We arrived at the wedding breakfast ten minutes late. About ten minutes after that a couple who are close friends of ours came in and sat next to us. The husband apologized. "I'm sorry we're late," he said. "We've been trapped in an elevator for forty minutes."

"Who rescued you?" asked Richard. "I wanted to know, too," said our friend. "We had been praying and signaling SOS for forty minutes, and I wanted to know who finally did something about it. The security man said the desk clerk at the hotel called."

Richard whispered to me, "You never know who you are going to save."

I can save life by not losing things, by not getting sick or having an accident, by liking change, by decreasing worry, by avoiding negative acts, and by eliminating self-defeating thoughts. I can enhance life by enjoying right now, by bearing burdens, by watering my neighbor's lawn, by anticipating good, and by responding to the unusual.

13

Independence
and Dependence

At a seminar on marriage I heard the statement that couples
are like two logs on a fire. When one gets cold the other is
there to get it warmed up and burning again. Good marriages
do just that. There are times I am mad at the world for no
real reason. Other times I feel unloved and depressed. At
these moments, the log I share a fire with puts his warm arms
around me and says something soothing or helpful or compli-
mentary which causes my kindling temperature to start rising
again. How grateful I've been at such times for the principle
of rubbing two sticks together to generate heat and ulti-
mately fire! Feelings of mutual trust, care, concern, and confidence generate the warmth that may eventually fuel the fire
of romance. Fire can be a friend. The energy which comes
from a burning substance lights a room, provides heat,

changes clay into pottery, drives machines, separates metals from ores, and keeps this planet green and populated.

One evening a friend of mine wanted to go to a lecture by an author who would only be speaking in town for one night. This author traveled about, speaking on a subject of great interest to my friend. Ordinarily there would have been nothing to stop her from going, but the day the lecture was to be held was her wedding anniversary. Her husband knew of her interest in the lecture but felt that celebrating their anniversary on their anniversary and doing what they traditionally did on anniversaries was more important.

My friend was disappointed and tried to get her husband to come with her to the lecture. But in the end, they went out to dinner and to see a play, much as they had done the preceding fifteen years. My friend felt slightly put out but reasoned that she should be celebrating her marriage with her partner, doing what he wanted to do. Reason sometimes has difficulty changing feelings, and my friend was struggling to be pleasant. But she dressed, cleaned the house, prepared the children's dinner, and had the babysitter there when her husband came home to pick her up. They drove to a favorite restaurant. When they had been seated, her husband handed her a prettily wrapped package. She opened it to find the latest book written by the author she had wanted to hear speak. She felt warmed. He did understand. She even enjoyed the play. Having someone to warm you is the nicest thing there is. That probably explains why marriage is so popular—about ninety-eight percent of the population tries it at least once.

Beneficial fire is wonderful. Yet, fire also can be an enemy. Uncontrolled fire chars marshmallows, burns toast, destroys homes, businesses, and relationships. Fire engulfs and devours. If beneficial fire is love, uncontrolled fire is anger and hate.

Those who have never married or are divorced or widowed no doubt sometimes wish for or miss a log beside them to have a little combustion with. Others, perhaps because of a bad experience, have played with fire enough and are happy to be the only burning ember in their lives. Some even feel fireproof—as if they will never again have the desire or ability to be set ablaze by another. There are others who never have shared the intimacy of a fire yet know how to absorb, reflect, and radiate. They may be candles, torches, two-hundred-watt globes, or lighthouses.

First

As cozy as the idea that marriage is like two logs on a fire sounds, I think it is inaccurate as a universal statement about marriage. Too many marriages have had fire hoses turned on them. It may appear as if one log from time to time does keep the other burning. However, too much dependence of one log on the other won't make a bonfire. If one only absorbs what the other radiates and gives nothing in return, there is usually not enough heat or light for a significant blaze. With the passage of time divorcées, widows, and never-marrieds may find the idea of two logs so appealing that they feel impoverished without that special log. The truth is, however, that we all need to look somewhere else for our source of light and heat. How many millions of logs have cozied up to some other log only to be tragically disappointed when they discover that there is not enough heat coming from the other log to keep the flame of marriage even flickering. If the analogy that one log keeps the other burning or needs another in order to burn were accurate, it would follow that if one log went out, the other would eventually die out too—which is not necessarily what happens. Also, arguably, if the logs stayed together they would eventually be consumed. That seldom happens. When one log goes out, the other of necessity rekindles itself and sometimes creates more of a blaze than the two did together.

Second

I think we are all singles regardless of marital status. We were born and will die alone. We think differently and in isolation from any other person. We are fully self-contained units with eyes, ears, tongues, appendages, ideas, personality, and past that are ours alone. We gain knowledge and testimony by ourselves. We receive ordinances, including a patriarchal blessing, as a single. The only exception to this is marriage, but even then we make promises alone. We all need two classifications—single-single, single-married, single-divorced, or single-widowed. In any of these situations we have the ability to be independent and to generate heat and light on our own. The focus of this book—keeping ourselves filled up and charged up—is one of the responsibilities we have as singles. If we become dying embers we need to find ways to rekindle ourselves and get burning again. Too much dependency causes low self-esteem. I believe the box we check—single, divorced, widowed, or married—has little to do with the BTUs we put out.

If our analogy of the fire is to be valid, we have to know that fire and the consequent light and heat don't just appear from nowhere. There has to be a continuous source from which we can draw. I once taught the eleven-year-old Merrie Miss girls in our ward. These are often cruel years for many girls. One of the girls was new to the neighborhood. She was pleased because one of the most popular girls in the neighborhood made friends with her immediately. The two of them did many things together, and the new girl felt warm and secure. A new school year was about to start. The morning of the first day of school the popular girl called the new girl to tell her that she would not be walking to school with her and that she hoped she would not follow her around, because she preferred to be with her old popular friends. Talk about flames being doused!

The next Primary day the new girl waited until the other girls had left the classroom. She told me what had happened and asked what she should do. I silently prayed for help. I asked the girl if she had thought about making new friends. She answered that all the girls seemed to have established friendships, and she was at best a tolerated third in each pair. I wondered what I should tell her. Finally I told her that as nice as friends are, she shouldn't count on them to make her feel good about herself. I told her about the concept of being your own best friend. She looked puzzled. I tried to explain. "If you go out searching for friendships in a panicked or desperate way, true friendship will continue to elude you. Have you ever chased a butterfly, trying and trying to catch it? It is more likely that if you would only stay still, it would light on your shoulder. If you prepare yourself for friendships, friendship will find you seemingly without effort. If you are first your own best friend, other friendships will follow.

"What do you mean?" she asked.

"What I'm trying to say is this: Make yourself the kind of person others will respect and desire to be around. As you do you will gain confidence in yourself. You will not need a popular friend to help you feel good about yourself. You will know you are a good, lovable, true friend, and others will want to be around you."

It would be nice if in life there were someone assigned to follow us around with bellows to help us when we are flickering. But think what a wonderful place this world would be if everyone was trying to do for himself whatever he could. We would put many counselors, psychologists, and psychiatrists out of work. Being your own best friend, being self-sufficient and independent, and generating your own light and heat and warmth bring blessings and fulfillment.

Third

The analogy of the logs and fire can be pressed one step further if we keep several points in mind. We need to remember that depending on another to keep us happy is unproductive and unfair; that we need to have the tools for combustion within ourselves rather than absorbing heat and light solely from others; that we have the ability to recharge ourselves, our self-esteem, our habits, our intensity for life; and that we are able to be single, whether married, widowed, divorced, or never-married. The goal is to be independent so we can be interdependent.

The scriptures help in expanding this analogy. Exodus 13:21, "And the Lord went before them by day in a pillar of a cloud, to lead them the way; and by night in a pillar of fire, to give them light." Psalm 27:1, "The Lord is my light." Psalm 36:9, "For with thee is the fountain of life: in thy light shall we see light." Isaiah 2:5, "O house of Jacob, come ye, and let us walk in the light of the Lord." Doctrine and Covenants 45:7, "For verily I say unto you that I am Alpha and Omega, the beginning and the end, the light and the life of the world—a light that shineth in darkness and the darkness comprehendeth it not." Ephesians 5:14, "Christ shall give thee light." Doctrine and Covenants 88:7-12, "This is the light of Christ. As also he is in the sun, and the light of the sun. . . .As also he is in the moon, and is the light of the moon . . . as also the light of the stars . . . and the earth also. . . .And the light which shineth, which giveth you light . . . which light proceedeth forth from the presence of God."

From these scriptures we understand that any light we have within us is from the Lord Jesus Christ. He is the light of the sun, moon, and stars, the light of the celestial, terrestrial, and telestial kingdoms. He is also the light of the world. He is my light and yours. If we need to be rekindled, if our flame is going out, if we are tired of always being our own best friend, we can go to Jesus Christ to be set ablaze again. Thus, marriage is not two logs dependently and passively lying side by side hoping the other will keep the flame of love alive. Rather, marriage is two strong single logs each radiating because it absorbs the light of Christ—doing as he would do, saying what he would say, keeping the commandments he has given. Strength and power to kindle ourselves or help another comes from the Source of Light.

Each of us will individually meet the Savior after this life. Another's merits will not help us meet and pass the test. I didn't send my Merrie Miss girl away after just telling her merely to be her own best friend. I told her that after she had done all she could for herself, there was someone who would be her best friend always—a friend who would always be there, a friend who would not leave her comfortless, a friend who would carry her burdens, a friend who died and was resurrected for her. No log will go out if Jesus is nearby. There can always be two logs on the fire if that other log is Jesus Christ, the Savior and the Light of the World. He alone can make up for the deficiencies we have. He can rekindle, reclaim, renew, restore, revitalize. "Come unto me, all ye that labour and are heavy laden, and I will give you rest. Take my yoke upon you, and learn of me; for I am meek and lowly in heart: and ye shall find rest unto your souls. For my yoke is easy, and my burden is light." (Matthew 11:28-30.) To him we will never be just a log on a fire.

14

Spiritual
Power

The older I grow the more I am of the opinion that the gospel is serious business. While in prison in Missouri Joseph Smith wrote to the Saints, "The things of God are of deep import; and time, and experience, and careful and ponderous and solemn thoughts can only find them out" (*Teachings of the Prophet Joseph Smith*, sel. Joseph Fielding Smith [Salt Lake City: Deseret Book Co., 1938], p. 137). I want to know the things of God. My relationship to him as I am being tested on this earth is the essence and purpose of my life. I am spending time and having many varied experiences. But am I learning the lessons he wants me to learn? Do I give careful, ponderous, and solemn thought to know the things of God? Not often enough.

Spirituality is a personal matter. Inner thought, desire,

motivation, and testimony levels are known only to ourselves and God. Since being spiritually full fills me as nothing else does, I begin the quest anew each morning. I try to set spiritual goals, but they are basically unmeasurable. For example, I set a goal to pray more sincerely. But do I pray in harmony with the Lord's will, with real intent, having faith in Christ? That's the way it is for me with each principle of the gospel. I'm never sure I measure up. Judging from conversations I've had with other women, I think you are much like me—truly desiring personal spiritual depth and reserves but not sure exactly how to attain this elusive goal. I can have a beautiful, spiritual experience one minute and the next be ordinary, old, telestial me.

The two spiritual qualities I most desire are to have the constant guidance of the Holy Ghost and to act as Jesus would.

The Still Small Voice

Reading the scriptures is one way I receive guidance from the Spirit. There are times I have been reading and an important piece of the spirituality puzzle has been put in place for me. My introduction to the word *unwearyingness* was one such experience. Another time I had a fascinating insight as a benefit of reading the scriptures. I wrote my thoughts about this occasion in the following verse:

Jarom

I'm too tired to read tonight.
"Oh, just one chapter,"
says a still, small voice.
Well, all right, where am I?
I think as I pull back the covers to sit on the edge.
Remembering
I turn the crinkly gold-rimmed pages past Enos.

I see another one-chapter book.
Good, only fifteen verses!
I begin:
The book of Jarom,
Son of Enos—
Receives revelations—
Prophesies—
Two hundred years have passed—
A now familiar cycle—
Righteous prosper, pride grows, sin abounds.
War.
Prophets preach, hearts mellow, repentance follows.
Peace.
Record ends, for plates are small.
Son Omni now to keep.
Pausing, the leather still between my hands,
a celestial panorama, unbidden,
lifts back the curtains of my mind.
I see glistening, white-robed beings.
"Come," my escort beckons.
Meekly following,
with naked feet on marbled floor,
we approach a group conversing.
Gesturing towards a heavenly man,
my escort says (after calling me by name),
"I would like you to meet Jarom."
Looking up to meet his gentle eyes, I whisper,
"I've read your book."

I have a friend who has struggled through many trials,
including numerous health problems and the death of a
child. As the straw that would break her, her husband con-
fessed he had committed a crime. He was a wonderful husband and father. How could he be sent to prison? She
anguished. The night before the sentencing, she fervently

prayed, asking that he be spared the indignities of prison. No answer seemed to come. Then she remembered stories of prayers being answered by opening the scriptures at random. She got up, opened her scriptures, and read the passage where her eyes first fell. "What, do ye suppose that mercy can rob justice? I say unto you, Nay; not one whit. If so, God would cease to be God." (Alma 42:25.) She dropped to her knees knowing two things—her husband would go to prison and, much more important, her Heavenly Father had heard her prayer and would help her endure.

The blessing of the Holy Ghost may also come as a result of another's response to promptings. A delicate, young bride told in fast and testimony meeting the story of the day she and her brother took her husband to the air force base so that he could leave for Saudi Arabia as part of Desert Shield. After their good-byes, her brother, a recently returned missionary, drove her to her apartment. She turned to him and said, "I can't go in. I can't live here alone. I am too afraid." Her brother told her she had no choice. "The apartment is close to your work and the ward. You'll be fine," he insisted. "I can't; I just can't," she cried. "I'll go in with you and make sure everything is OK," he said. They went into the apartment together. He looked around and then knelt down by the sofa. She knelt beside him. Then, by the power of the priesthood he honored, he blessed the apartment that it would be a safe haven for her during her husband's absence. He asked that the Holy Ghost would protect the apartment, and that his sister would not be or feel alone. As she bore her testimony, the tears choked her voice as she said, "And every time I enter the apartment, the Spirit is there waiting to welcome me home."

Like Elijah, I have looked for answers in the wind, earthquake, and fire. I've wanted overpowering, precise answers written on Belshazzar's wall. There have been depressed, humble hours when I have cried, "Where are you? I need your help. Show me the way and I'll go; tell me what to do and I'll do it." On better days I have prayed, "Please guide me with thy Spirit. I want to be of service. Help me be at the right place at the right time." Then I usually get busy and forget the lesson of Elijah and the still small voice.

A mother in our ward had just lost custody of her children. It was Mother's Day. I wondered how she could come to sacrament meeting on this day, but there she was. In Primary we had had a fun Mother's Day program. Each child had given a corsage to his or her mother. I had one left over. During the meeting I felt I should turn around. I saw this woman sitting on the back row, dabbing at her eyes. As I turned back around I saw the corsage. I knew what I was to do. The minute the amen of the closing prayer was said, I grabbed the corsage and ran to the back of the room. She was already out of the chapel and near the back door of the building. I knew she didn't want to talk or let anyone see her. I grabbed her arm. She turned to see who was stopping her quick exit. Without words I pinned the corsage on her. She hugged me tightly. We cried together. A few days later I received this note:
"Dear Sister Linford:

"You really touched me on Mother's Day. I'm sorry I fell apart, but I'm sure you understand. I did want you to know that you gave me strength, and later on that day I was able to be in tune to another and lift her up. I had a wonderful day!"

She realized it was not me but the Spirit who had helped her. She was lifted and able later to lift another. I was lifted by her response, but more than that, the Spirit had given me a job to do. I can't think of a higher honor than being trusted by the Spirit. I pray that I will listen intently so that the voice of the Holy Ghost will be neither too still nor too small for me to hear it.

Everything Within His Power

We often check out from the ward library the Genesis

Project videos of the life of Christ. The actor who portrays Jesus in the videos is caring and in charge. He acts like a leader. He responds to people positively—with a smile, a knowing look, or a simple touch. As he walks through crowds he moves with purpose, energy, and power. I keep that portrayal of Jesus in my mind as I read the New Testament, and I feel as if I am present during his ministry. I have seen him raise Jairus's daughter from her death bed. I have seen him rise magnificently from sleep on a small ship on a raging Sea of Galilee to calm his creations. I have seen him give sight to the blind. I have seen him nailed to a cross and laid in a tomb. I have then rejoiced as the smiling, knowing Savior shows his nail-printed hands to his disciples. I have pleaded, with the men on the road to Emmaus, "Abide with me."

I have wondered, as I make decisions and work through problems in my own life, how Jesus would respond. I wanted to know how he would act or what he would do in various situations so that I could teach our children how to be like Jesus. I searched for an answer children would understand. But how could I presume to understand the mind of deity? One day I was thinking about the differences in our abilities—his and mine. It was a fast day and I felt weak. I thought about his forty-day fast. I felt as if I could survive only a few more hours without food. It was not within my power to fast even two days. Somewhere along this trail of thought a simple answer to my question came. How could every child and adult be like Jesus? The answer was that Jesus responded to others' needs according to his knowledge, maturity, and power levels.

So, I can be like Jesus if I respond to others according to my knowledge, maturity, and power. That means I can be me. I don't have to be perfect. I don't have to respond as you would; I don't have to compare myself to anyone else. If I happen to be ill on a certain day, I can respond within those limits. Perhaps saying thanks is as close as I can get to being like Jesus at that moment. If I am pregnant or suffering from PMS or postpartum depression, all I have to do is that which is within my power at that moment. I don't need to feel guilty for not doing more.

Following the example of the Good Samaritan is an easy way to start being like Jesus. Husbands, children, neighbors, and strangers need us to stop and take notice of them and help them according to our power. I had an experience on the freeway that affirmed this idea. Around six-thirty one evening I saw a woman about my age leave her stalled car on the freeway and begin to walk. I saw three cars pull off to help her. A single man was in each car. I slowed down to see what would happen. She refused help from each. By then I was too far ahead to safely stop. I took the closest exit and came around again. She was still walking. I pulled over and asked how I could help. I had five children and as many pizzas in the car. She surveyed us, thanked us, and got in the car. I did not pay for her gas or car repair. I did not buy her a meal or pay for any lodging. I was able to be a Good Samaritan because I was a woman with children and because I was in the right place at the right time. I did what was within my power at that moment.

How can we do as Jesus did when he calmed the wind and sea? We do not have his power over the elements, but we do have the power to calm, perhaps, our own nerves, a crying baby, contentious children, a disheartened sister, or an overworked husband. It is within our power to find solutions, to work through difficult situations, to be peacemakers. We don't have the power to say, "Peace, be still," and have everything in commotion suddenly become quiet. But we do have the power, with the help of time, to calm and bring peace to ourselves and those in our sphere. This task may be as simple as giving someone a smile or as difficult as patiently helping another work through a serious problem.

How can we do as Jesus did when he brought sight to the

blind? Do we have the power to help others see? Yes, it is within our power to help a child "see" to choose the right. We can be missionaries by example and precept to help others "see" the truths of the gospel. We can let others "see" our good works so that they will glorify our Father which is in heaven.

Jesus worked within his power. Can we do as he did when he raised the son of the widow of Nain from his casket? Is it within our power to give life? In a sense, yes. We can assist in giving life to God's creations as we work in our gardens and yards. We can help give life as we give birth and/or nurture God's children. We can take part in giving eternal life to ourselves as we keep the commandments and accept the Atonement. We can give the opportunity for eternal life to others as we do genealogical research. We can give ourselves and others longer life by learning the laws of nutrition and by feeding our families accordingly. Our likeness to Jesus will come as we try to do as he did, subject to the parameters of our own power.

I like the story of the evil lawyer who fell in love with the pure and beautiful country girl. She would not marry him unless he reformed. She said she wanted to marry someone who had the face of a saint. He went to a mask maker who fashioned an undetectable mask that depicted his features in a saintly appearance. He married the girl, repented, and spent his time doing good. Years later some old acquaintances who were part of his former deceptions wanted to reveal his crimes. In a violent act they ripped the mask from his face. He thought his world had come to an end—that his wife and children would disown him. He asked for a mirror to see the face that had been hidden beneath the mask. To his amazement his reflection showed the face he had grown used to seeing. He had the face of a saint.

As we desire and try to live close to the Holy Ghost, as our gospel knowledge increases and we mature in the ability to serve, doing everything within our power to be like Jesus, our faces and lives will radiate his image and we will become more spiritual. We will feel more fulfilled and filled up. We have the promise that this will happen. "Blessed are they which do hunger and thirst after righteousness: for they shall be filled" (Matthew 5:6).

15

The End and
the Beginning

In the beginning we asked what word would best complete the following analogy: Fuel is to the car as _____ is to the woman. I've worried, through these many pages, that there isn't a word that really fits. At the end of each chapter the blank could be filled with the subject of that particular chapter. Fuel is to the car as celebrations, or unwearyingness, or spiritual power are to the woman. But I like things to be simple; I want one word. I made a list of possible choices— accomplishment, achievement, realization, fruition, completion, contentment, happiness, peace of mind, satisfaction— but not one expresses the complete idea. I want a word which embodies all the qualities of my ambitions and potential. I want a word that describes the total feeling I have when any of the things I have promised, planned for, desired,

accomplished, expected, hoped for, or prayed for become
realities. I thought of the theme of being filled and fulfilled.
Then I thought of the noun form of one of these words—*fulfillment*. What do you think? Fuel is to the car as fulfillment
is to the woman. I think it will do. The good thing about this
word is that it takes into account the facts that the recipe for
fulfillment is different for every woman, and that what con-
stitutes fulfillment for a particular woman may vary with different seasons and cycles.

I had yet another experience with a car. It was Halloween and twenty-one degrees outside. I had to buy apple
cider, dry ice, and name tags and be at Daniel's fifth grade
class by two-fifteen. At noon my plan was to run a few
errands, stop by the store, and be at the school on time. On
my way to complete the first errand, I was about two miles
from home when I rounded a corner and the right front tire
of the car blew out. I thought of changing it myself, but I
knew the weather was just too cold. I decided to walk home
and call for help. Since I hadn't planned on a two-mile walk,
I was wearing a light jacket over a sweat suit. When I opened
the trunk to make sure there was a spare tire, I saw that our
sixteen-year-old Christine's old winter coat happened to be
in the trunk. On the way home I thought about my recipe for
fulfillment at any particular moment. How grateful I was that
I was driving rather than one of our teenagers! I was grateful
I was traveling twenty miles per hour and not sixty-five. I
was thankful I got a flat tire close enough to home to walk.
And, oh, how thankful I was for that old coat!

Lori, my sister-in-law, lives in Houston, Texas. She is the
mother of four children under the age of seven and is a Relief
Society president. Two weeks after her last baby was born,
she needed to be at homemaking meeting in seconds, and
the meetinghouse was twenty minutes away. She backed
down their curved driveway to find that her husband had left
his car at the bottom of the driveway. She discovered this by

hitting his car. Oh, well, two cars with dented fenders. She proceeded on to the meeting but soon saw blue and red lights flashing behind her. The ticket she received was for going sixty-five in a forty-five-mile-an-hour zone. The homemaking meeting went fine. Then she came home to hear the baby crying and see that the sprinklers were still on. She ran in the house, grabbed the baby, and went outside to turn off the sprinklers. She saw something moving toward her, and before she knew what was happening a skunk had sprayed her and the baby. Lori is a woman who felt fulfilled enough to laugh and laugh as she shared the story.

I have a friend whose husband is being consumed by cancer. I asked her if fulfillment is possible for her in this most difficult time. She looked at me as though I knew nothing. "Of course," she said. "When I watch him struggle to stand straight enough to see in the bathroom mirror, when I fight to maintain some composure at his early retirement party, when I hear the grim diagnosis that the cancer is now in yet another location, I think I can hardly endure. But then I kneel beside his bed each night for our prayer. I hear him thank his Father for this day. I hear him thank the Lord for providing him with a loving wife and family and skillful doctors. I hear him thank the Lord that he was chosen to be so afflicted rather than a brother or sister. I hear him ask for a blessing of health to be given to this or that person in the family, ward, or neighborhood—people who have very minor ailments compared to his. If this weren't such a terrible ordeal, I would say it is a most enriching time of our lives. And, yes, I do feel fulfilled."

It is my goal and hope and prayer that whether we are enduring the bother of a flat tire, the inconvenience of dented fenders, a traffic ticket, and skunk smell, the hurdle of terminal cancer, or any of the ups and downs in between, we will find fulfillment.

This is the end of the book but the beginning of the continuing quest to be a woman fulfilled.

Index